Scholarships

101

DATE DUE

Scholarships
101

The Real-World Guide to Getting Cash for College

Kimberly Stezala

AMACOM

American Management Association

New York • Atlanta • Brussels • Chicago • Mexico City • San Francisco
Shanghai • Tokyo • Toronto • Washington, D.C.

Special discounts on bulk quantities of AMACOM books are
available to corporations, professional associations, and other
organizations. For details, contact Special Sales Department,
AMACOM, a division of American Management Association,
1601 Broadway, New York, NY 10019.
Tel.: 212-903-8316.   Fax: 212-903-8083.
E-mail: specialsls@amanet.org
Website: www.amacombooks.org/go/specialsales
To view all AMACOM titles go to www.amacombooks.org

This publication is designed to provide accurate and authoritative information in regard to the subject
matter covered. It is sold with the understanding that the publisher is not engaged in rendering legal,
accounting, or other professional service. If legal advice or other expert assistance is required, the
services of a competent professional person should be sought.

All information and opinions shared by the author are not to be construed as legal or financial
advice. The author's methods and opinions are not necessarily endorsed by the individuals or
organizations mentioned in the text. The author makes no representation or warranty of the
accuracy or completeness of the information, makes no guarantee that participants will win
scholarships, and accepts no liability.

Various words and phrases used by companies to distinguish their goods and services from others
can be protected intellectual property. AMACOM and the author use such words and phrases in
this book for editorial purposes only, with no intention of violating the intellectual property of such
companies. All such words and phrases are set out in initial Capital Letters or ALL CAPITAL
letters. Individual companies should be contacted for complete information regarding their
respective intellectual property and its permitted use.

The Scholarship Lady^{SM}, Team of Champions™, Fabulous Factor™, Scholarship Success Boot
Camp^{SM} and the Dream, Plan, Act, Excel™ method are trademarks and service marks of Stezala
Consulting, LLC.

Library of Congress Cataloging-in-Publication Data

Stezala, Kimberly.
    Scholarships 101 : the real-world guide to getting cash for college / Kimberly Stezala.
        p.   cm.
    Includes index.
    ISBN 978-0-8144-0981-7 (pbk.)
    1. Scholarships—United States.   2. Universities and colleges—United States—Admission.
    I. Title.   II. Title: Scholarships one hundred one.   III. Title: Scholarships one hundred and one.
    LB2338.S82 2008
    378.3'4—dc22

                                                            2008012097

Printing number

10 9 8 7 6 5 4 3 2 1

Contents

Acknowledgments

My mom has been telling me since grade school that I would write a book; not should, or could, but *would*. She also showed me that helping other people was part of our family fiber. If you combine those constants with my scholarship knowledge, you have *Scholarships 101*. Thanks, Mom.

I was blessed to have more than my mom on my side. Hundreds of people, including students, parents, guidance counselors, scholarship sponsors, college administrators, and precollege practitioners, helped me crystallize the need for a new kind of scholarship book. To the students who always told the truth, which is underappreciated today, I thank you for your honesty. Thank you to all of the folks who hosted Scholarship Success Boot Camps or reviewed my ideas along the way. Maria, Tanya, Krista, Patricia, and Barbara, I am grateful for your support.

Special acknowledgment is due to those of you who shared your personal stories or expertise in the book. We all grow a little wiser by reading your firsthand accounts. Thank you so much for sharing and for your willingness to help college-bound students. I hope you, your families, and your organizations flourish. To the members and staff of the National Scholarship Providers Association, your work is an inspiration.

Thank you to my parents Cindy, Al, Carolyn, and Gary, my brother Nick and his family, my in-laws Bonnie and Don, and to

Jenny, who just finished college. A special thanks to Debbie—your gift forced me to write.

In the writing world, I must thank Jean Rabe, Carolyn Washburne, and Judy Bridges; the writers at Redbird; and my compatriots at Absolute Write, for sage advice.

Thank you to my agent Sharlene Martin and AMACOM's Jacquie Flynn. You saw what I was hoping you would see. I realize I wouldn't be here writing this page if it weren't for you. I very much appreciate the roles of Erika Spelman, Barry Richardson, Jennifer Holder, Alice Northover, and the staff at AMACOM. You gave me every reason to love the publishing world. You also created a deeper sense of humility in my life as a writer. Thanks.

My Team of Champions at home deserves more praise than I can imagine. To my young ones, I hope when it's your turn to prepare for college, you'll understand my sense of duty and forgive me for working until midnight too many times. You are my inspiration and I thank you for all the sacrifices you made. I could only write this book knowing you were in good hands. To my hubby Darren, who told me every step of the way, "You can do it"; rubbed my shoulders when they ached; tolerated my deadline-driven behavior; convinced the kids to step away from my office door; and read, proofread, and critiqued the manuscript with a characteristic calm, I love you for all of that and more. Thank you.

Scholarships
101

Introduction

Y ou are the primary reason I wrote this book. Whether you are a parent, student, counselor, mentor, big sister, grandfather, teacher, or youth minister, I want you to know everything I know about scholarships.

I know that the cost of college continues to rise faster than inflation, costs more than a loaded luxury car, and petrifies college-bound students of modest means. I am often called upon to teach workshops or give speeches to college-bound students and their families, and I do this with joy because I see so many people who could go to college but don't have the money and don't understand how to secure scholarships. Or, maybe they have a little bit of money saved for college but not the tens of thousands of dollars it costs to earn a degree. This book is for all of you.

I want you to learn about essay writing, gratitude, organization, and marketing. I want you to help your neighbor, friend, or co-worker. I want you to understand that winning scholarships is possible.

But if you read the book and just do as I say, that will be a big disappointment to me. Interaction is an important part of using this book. I know that students do not learn best by reading but by doing, discussing, and incorporating the material into their reality. I have seen it at my Scholarship Success Boot Camps^{SM}. In the best-case scenario, you will not hoard this information but gather a few friends, read your essays together,

1

proofread one another's work, and pass along good scholarship leads. You will build your own team of people who serve as champions in your quest for scholarships. Everyone from your grandma to your best friend will have a role in your success.

I am especially inspired by the people I interviewed for the book. The students, sponsors, and parents who confirmed my hunches or shed new light on what it's like to be them are all motivated, caring people who really want to help others be successful in winning scholarships. They devoted their time to tell you in their own words what it takes to win. Heed their advice.

As you begin to incorporate *Scholarships 101* into your life, I encourage you to set your own goals and personalize the Dream, Plan, Act, and Excel™ methods introduced in the book. The meaning will be different for you than for a student from a different background. You might have a 3.8 grade point average, excel at all of your extracurricular activities, and attend a school with a sophisticated, helpful guidance department—or, you might not. In my fifteen years of helping students attain their educational dreams, I worked primarily with urban public and private schools. Based on what I experienced, I realized that not every student has the same support system or resources available on the pathway to college. If a student's parents did not attend college, he or she faces even more obstacles in navigating financial aid, college applications, and yes, scholarships. *Scholarships 101* acknowledges variances in student preparation and student support, and it provides tools and exercises to equip *all* students to succeed. I learn new things every day to help students, and you can visit www.scholarshipstreet.com, the companion website of this book, to download new tools and resources.

The point of *Scholarships 101* is to the take the best advice on winning scholarships and to teach you how to make it your own. Think of it as an introductory course combined with independent study. My job is not to tell you what to do, *but to teach you how to create your own plan for scholarship success*, based on your reality. Are you ready?

Meet Your New Neighbor

"**A**re you the Scholarship Lady?" the young woman asked me as I pushed my shopping cart into the checkout lane. "Yes," I replied, preparing myself for the barrage of questions that usually followed. Similar interactions have happened at libraries, grocery stores, and family restaurants. When it comes to free advice, especially about paying for college, people aren't shy about asking questions. Moms approach me as they search their purses for a scrap of paper to jot down tips or a website address. High school seniors give me a nod in the hallway and stop to say hi. Relatives and old friends, who now have kids in high school, come over for a cup of coffee and stay for financial aid advice.

The Scholarship Lady℠

Why do they approach me—a person who has never won a scholarship? Because they trust me, they know I've helped other families, and they know I care.

I wish someone had given me scholarship advice during my senior year of high school in 1987. Back then, I applied for one scholarship from a women's club and didn't win. No one in my family knew how to help me, and the only books available were two-pound directories that listed thousands of scholarships in microscopic type. I went into information overload and never filled out another scholarship application. What I did learn over the years, as a result of my career, was how to break down the information to help other students succeed.

If you are motivated to go to college and have somewhat decent grades (a 2.5 grade point average or better), you can make it to college with some money to pay the bill. I can show you how.

My goal is to help you win scholarships. Why should you listen to me? Because I have devoted my career to helping families achieve their educational dreams. I have worked with scholarship programs, universities, libraries, schools, and community organizations to help students make it to college. I was also the manager of an online scholarship database in Wisconsin, where we researched, analyzed, and promoted more than $3 million in available scholarships. Throughout this process, I had the privilege to meet the people who had the money and, more important, the people who needed the money—like you. I saw the best- and worst-case scenarios from the donors' and students' perspectives. I also learned how to write successful proposals to gain funding for our programs. Learning how to write successful proposals, or in your case, scholarship applications, is definitely doable and I will show you how.

You may have seen books written by outstanding college students who tout strategies for winning scholarship money. As the director of a college-preparation program in Wisconsin, my staff and I were aware of these books but rarely used them when advising students. First, they seemed too long. Who wants to read 300 or more pages to get the information that he or she needs? I don't, nor do students or parents who are pressed for time. Another drawback was the lack of attention these books gave to parents and other family members.

Our students were oftentimes the first in their families to go to college and most weren't headed for Harvard. Our students had decent grades and planned to attend college, but their families needed advice on how to prepare for it or how to pay for it.

This convinced me that people needed street-smart advice on how average families and their high school students could find money for college. I also knew that many qualified students skipped applying for scholarships because they lacked confidence, knowledge, or support.

Maybe no one in your family has gone to college. Maybe you're not wealthy enough to pay cash for college and not broke enough to qualify for income-based grants. Maybe you have moderate financial resources but not enough to cover the cost of expected tuition, books, housing, transportation, and everything else you need to go to college. Most likely, you will qualify for student loans but are petrified about being in debt after earning your degree. You are, as we say in the financial aid business, "stuck in the middle." *Scholarships 101* is for you.

I promise to share all of my neighborly advice and tell you the real-world version of getting scholarships in a simple "101" style. Think of it as a kitchen-table classroom where the whole family is enrolled.

What Does *101* Mean?

When you begin college, your first classes are likely to be "100 level" courses, or introductory courses, for a subject. Likewise, *Scholarships 101* is primarily for high school students who are college-bound and seeking scholarships for the first time. Parents, friends, neighbors, teachers, advisors, and counselors are welcome, too!

Recipe for Success

What makes a recipe great is fine ingredients and proper preparation. Your recipe for scholarship success includes four key ideas that I will refer to throughout the book: Dream, Plan, Act, and Excel. What does this cryptic recipe mean? Let's talk about it.

Dream

What are your dreams for the future? For you to be successful, you need to dream big so that the little monotonous tasks have a purpose. How will you make it to medical school? How in the world are you going to pay $20,000 tuition every year? When that stack of scholarship applications begins to intimidate you, how will you overcome your fear? Do you have enough stamps to mail your applications?

If you don't have a dream, it is difficult to succeed, because you focus on the lowest common denominator and can be easily discouraged. You focus on passing a class instead of getting an A. You focus on graduating from high school instead of going to college. You focus on getting a job instead of finding a career. Get the picture? I will talk about "dreaming big" throughout the book. Your dream will help motivate you throughout the scholarship search and application process.

Plan

Do you have a plan? I am aware that many students say they want to go to college, but for a small percentage their actions don't follow their dreams. According to the National Center for Education Statistics, in 2002 about 80 percent of tenth graders expected to obtain a bachelor's degree or higher, but for seniors in 2005, only 69 percent actually enrolled in college in the fall after graduation. Why? Maybe they weren't prepared emotionally, academically, or financially. Maybe they weren't wealthy. According to the 2006 report "Promise Abandoned" by The Education Trust, low-achieving, high-income students go to college at the same rate as high-achieving, low-income students. This doesn't seem fair, but the point is that the more money you have, the more choices you have.

This book will help you create a plan of how to win scholarship money to help pay for the cost of college. I'm assuming you do not have a scholarship plan yet and that is why you are reading this book. The plan is directly tied to your dream. See where I'm going here?

Act

What will you need to succeed? You will need to act on your dream and your plan. If it is your senior year of high school, you might be thinking, "What can I do now? Is it too late?" No matter what stage you are at, you can always take action. Some people make the mistake of doing more without doing better. For example, if you sign up for the forensics team, Earth club, church choir, and the prom committee all in the same semester, you are definitely doing more. Your actions are altruistic, but my advice is to join more activities only if you can fully participate and prove your positive impact.

In essence, I'm simply asking you to act on your intentions and your word. If you promise your teacher that you will share your résumé so she can write a good, personalized letter of recommendation for you, will you do it? I hope so. Proactive students are likely to find more scholarships. In *Scholarships 101*, you won't sit around waiting for someone to hand you a list of scholarships; you will make your own list—you will act on the need to personalize your scholarship approach. By the way, reading this book is very proactive!

Excel

The old saying "spinning your wheels" means you're stepping on the gas but not moving. In the world of scholarships, some advisors will tell you to apply for as many scholarships as you can. My advice is to apply for as many scholarships as you can *if you can excel at what you do and can submit high-quality, compelling applications.* If you crank out a bunch of mediocre applications, then you're doing more work but it is not necessarily your best work. You can't afford to be mediocre when applying for scholarships, because the competition is at an all-time high due to the increasing number of college applicants who need financial aid. But don't worry, with this book, you will learn how to excel beyond the competition.

Neighborly Advice from Your Instructor

Do you have good friends or family members who feel at home in your house? When friends visit my house, they know to come right in and help themselves in the fridge. If someone rings the doorbell, I know right away it is a salesperson who is peddling magazines or a new, amazing, all-purpose cleaner. Please consider me the no-doorbell, open-fridge type of neighbor who happens to be your scholarship instructor.

Here are some tips for getting the most out of *Scholarships 101*:

- ■ The 101 symbol marks special advice from students, sponsors, me, and other experts.
- ■ The $ indicates the beginning of profiles of people who have been successful or scholarship-winning tips from people who know the field.

- ■ "Quick Terms" define words or concepts that may be new to you. A full glossary is in appendix C, but it is much more helpful to have the words right where you need them.

- ■ The "Fridge Notes" summaries will keep your whole family organized, motivated, and focused. Copy them from the book or print from the website for your personal use and put them up on your refrigerator for everyone to see.

- ■ Visit www.scholarshipstreet.com—the official website for this book. It is your hub for tools and samples to assist you in achieving scholarship success.

- ■ Bring your family and friends, because the bell is about to ring.

Quick Terms

Financial Aid: All forms of financial assistance awarded to your family to help pay for college.

Grants: Financial aid that does not need to be paid back. State, federal, tribal, and institutional grants are most common. Grants may be based on your income level, academic standing, race, ethnicity, or other qualifying factors. You may need to apply for grants or they may be awarded to you automatically if you meet the criteria.

Scholarships: Financial aid that is awarded to you based on your individual characteristics. Scholarships are the wildcard of financial aid and do not have to be paid back. The sponsors can set their own criteria, deadlines, and application process. It is up to you to find scholarships that match your profile and to submit a winning application.

Student Loans: Financial aid that is offered to you based on the shortfall between what you have and what you owe toward the cost of college. Loans accrue interest and must be repaid.

Chapter 2

Invest in the Best—You!

You are the best you. No one else can compete with that. However, when you stack yourself up against hundreds of other students, how do you compare? When it comes to scholarships, the cliché "everyone's a winner" does not apply.

Leave Luck in the Dust

Think of it this way: only one team wins the Super Bowl, one singer becomes the American Idol, and one politician wins the election. Winning is a combination of talent, preparation, perseverance, and luck. The same is true of scholarships. The best strategy is to focus on talent, preparation, and perseverance, and leave luck in the dust!

You cannot ensure that all scholarship judges will have had a good cup of coffee before they review your application, but you can ensure the level of preparation you put into your studies, volunteer work, and scholarship applications. Why would a scholarship committee want to spend its cash on you if you haven't invested in yourself? What do you think of yourself? What do others think of you? The adults around you will be very important in supporting your quest for scholarships, and you must prove to them that you are serious. How do you prove that you are a worthy investment? Your track record and your intentions will be an indicator.

Your Past and Present

Throughout the college-enrollment and scholarship-application process, you will rely on written words and statistical information to prove your worth. Except for sports, art, and music, very few scholarships have tryouts, scouting, or auditions. Your paper trail and documentation of success is crucial. How do you document your success? The most basic form of documentation is your transcript, which is your school district's official record of your grades. Scholarship sponsors may ask for a copy of it to ensure that your memory of getting an A in calculus is accurate. Your transcripts should show that you took progressively more challenging classes and had decent grades along the way.

The majority of private scholarships are merit-based scholarships. This means they are based on academic achievement. Although you don't need a 4.0 grade point average to win scholarships, you do need to prove that you are a worthy use of the sponsor's money. Because the judges don't know you, they are going to want proof of your academic performance, such as ACT or SAT standardized test scores, your cumulative grade point average, and your enrollment in college-preparation classes. Additional factors might be your grades in Advanced Placement courses, inclusion on the honor roll, and teachers' recommendations. Every scholarship is different, and it is up to you to take note of the requirements.

Scholarship providers also want "well-rounded" students. What does that mean? It means that in addition to having decent grades, you have shown involvement or interest in other activities. Many students make the mistake of overenrolling in activities just to boost their résumés. It is more important to focus on fewer interests and excel at them. You want to win awards for participation and exhibit leadership skills in the activities that appeal to you. High school is a time to explore your interests, but if you are still hopping from group to group during your senior year, it will appear that you lack focus.

Another part of your past is your involvement in your neighborhood, community, or place of worship. Volunteer work and impact on the community are increasingly being used as qualifiers for scholarships. Scholarship providers might allow you to substitute work experience for volunteer experience if you can prove that you learned something valuable such as how to be on time, respectful, or responsible. If you must work to help your family pay the bills or save up for college, you can weave that into the scholarship application essay or cover letter.

Now that we've talked about your past, let's take a look at the present. Your personal investment could include studying more, participating in tutoring, building better relationships with teachers, promoting yourself to counselors (do they know who you are?), or other self-centered tasks. It is a necessity to be self-centered at this time. Your friends will forgive you, and they can't help you pay for college, can they? Let's break it down together year by year so you can see if you are on track and where you might need to invest in yourself.

Ninth Grade/Freshman Year

As a freshman you are probably trying to figure out where you fit in. Take time to try new things and make the most of everything that your high school can offer. If you want to attend college, you must focus on doing your best and it all starts here.

Researchers often use algebra grades as a predictor for college enrollment. In other words, if you earned a B or better in Algebra I, you are more likely to go to college than students who earned a C or below. If you earned a C or below in algebra, did you improve as you moved ahead? Did you do better in geometry or maintain a B or better in other classes? To be clear, it's not solely about the algebra, it's about those students possessing a trait that makes them more likely to succeed. When I conducted research with college-bound students at a local high school, I found the same correlation. The point is to stay strong freshman year so you have something to build upon. Say it with me: stay strong.

Quick Terms

Standardized Tests: Tests meant to measure your college readiness in terms of your level of achievement or aptitude. The ACT and SAT are the major tests. The test scores may be used by colleges during the admissions process and by scholarship providers during the application process.

Tenth Grade/Sophomore Year

As a sophomore, you should focus on mastering the basics of core courses so you can take advanced courses in the years ahead. You should be preparing for standardized tests such as the SAT or ACT and might consider taking the Preliminary SAT/ National Merit Scholarship Qualifying Test (PSAT/NMSQT) or the PLAN tests, which will help you determine your level of college readiness. These tests are precursors to the SAT or ACT tests that you will take in junior or senior year.

You have many choices for test prep: online, in class, at a college, through a book, or through a tutoring agency. Test prep will help you understand what the test is like, will help you hone your skills, and will help you get comfortable with time-crunched test taking.

What if your family doesn't have the money for test-prep classes? Ask your counselor if anyone in town offers free test prep. In my town, an African-American women's club holds free test prep on Saturday mornings, and several colleges offer low- or no-cost classes for lower-income students. Your school may also offer waivers or mini-scholarships to pay for the test-preparation classes.

This is a good time to explore careers that might interest you. Your school should conduct occupational assessments to help you determine your interests. You basically answer several dozen questions about your likes and dislikes, and this creates a profile about careers that are matched to your traits. I have worked with hundreds of sophomores in taking these tests and most of the time the tests are pretty accurate, but I'll admit that some students didn't strike me as future ballerinas, as the results indicated.

You can also visit your local library and ask where you can find career information. The Internet is also full of career-exploration websites, but it can be overwhelming to do this alone. Find someone to help you, even if it's after school. In a friendly, sincere voice ask people you admire, "How did you get this job?" Even if you don't know them, you can still ask. Most adults will be thrilled to tell you all about their paths to success. As a courtesy, be prepared to listen to a few long-winded explanations about the "good old days" and try to glean the best advice.

Professional groups and associations are eager to support enthusiastic students who want to pursue certain careers. You could be an architect, teacher, or health care professional, but how will you know if these fields are a good match if you don't investigate the possibilities?

Eleventh Grade/Junior Year

Your junior year of high school is as important as your senior year. Many students underestimate the importance of junior year. Your junior-year course selection, grades, and experiences will be the basis for your *college* applications, and many colleges use your enrollment application as your *scholarship* application. Although this saves time for the college admissions staff and prevents you from filling out multiple scholarship applications, be absolutely sure that your unique characteristics are apparent to them.

Have you taken more than the minimum requirements to graduate? Remember your plan for success includes doing more and doing better. Have you taken the ACT or SAT yet? If you are not happy with the results, you should invest in test-preparation classes, books, and tutoring. After the test, you will receive a score report. You and your family should determine if retaking the test will improve your scores. The majority of students who study and retake the test do in fact improve their scores.

Scholarship judges are savvy enough to understand that sometimes even straight-A students have text anxiety and do not perform well on tests. If that is the case, remember, your main proof of academic achievement consists of your grades and your transcript.

Bonus Answers

How is it possible to get the answers to the SAT or ACT without cheating? You'll have to wait until after the test!

Seriously, both testing companies offer an extra service that shows you which questions you got wrong, the answers you provided, and the correct answers for those questions. *If you take your tests very early*, this may be a worthwhile service for you. *Caution*: It can take four to six weeks after you get your test scores to receive the extra service report, depending on the service. This may not be ample time to study, register, and retake the test on the next scheduled date, but it may be enough time for the test scheduled after that one. For example, if you take the test in December and order this service, you may not have time to receive, review, and study for the next test in April. You would, however, have time to study for the test in June.

I only advocate signing up for this bonus service *if you will have time to use the results to study and improve your score* or, if like me, you're just curious about what the right answers were. Many students will retake the ACT or SAT, but what if they never learned the material properly in the first place? Or they make the same mistakes twice? Although your second test will not include the exact same questions as your first test, you will learn the subject matter better if you know what went wrong.

According to ACT and SAT, the demand for this service has increased over the last several years. If you choose to order this service, you can do so when you take the test or after you get your score report back. If you order it when you take the test, you will receive the results sooner than if you wait. The bottom line? If you have the extra money and have enough time to use the results, reflect, and study, it's worth considering.

Here's the scoop:

Test	Name of Service	Fees	Details	Website
ACT	Test Information Release (TIR)	$16.00, subject to change.	Read ACT's registration materials and website for information about this service. It is only offered on certain test dates.	www.act.org
SAT	Question-and-Answer Service (QAS)	$18.00, subject to change.	*Applies to SAT Reasoning Test only.* Read SAT's registration materials and website for information about this service. It is only offered on certain test dates.	www.collegeboard.com

What else should you do in junior year? Begin to take leadership roles in school activities (if seniors will let you)! If you and a few friends have a passion that is not represented on your campus, think about starting your own club. Are you into computer programming, saving the environment, or salsa dancing? If you can find an advisor such as a teacher, coach, counselor, or parent who shares your passion or is willing to supervise your group, go for it.

Have you ever thought of starting your own business? Would you be good at detailing cars, caring for lawns, fixing computers, sewing purses, or being a DJ? These entrepreneurial pursuits will help you earn money for college and prove to scholarship judges that you are motivated.

Working for free, also called volunteering, service learning, interning, and community service, is another option to round out your junior year. If you haven't "given back to the community," you had better start immediately because most scholarship sponsors want to give their money to civic-minded students. Let it be you. Who in town needs your help? Whether it's the local YMCA, food pantry, recreation department, nursing home, or your neighborhood elementary school, these places can only thrive through the generosity of volunteers.

Another bonus is that these organizations may offer scholarships of their own. For instance, the Boys & Girls Clubs of Greater Milwaukee (my town) awards at least three scholarships each year for seniors who participated as members or volunteers and had a 2.0 or above grade point average. How hard is that? As another bonus, volunteering will connect you to new people in a variety of careers. You might meet social workers, nurses, accountants, writers, and so many other professionals. Pick your passion and check it out.

Do you know your guidance counselor? If your school is similar to most, where the counselors are assigned hundreds of students, your counselor may have forgotten your name. Unless, of course, you are a stellar student or a prankster. If you go to class regularly, maintain a B average, and choose the suggested courses, you might not stand out. You need to stand out. When it comes to scholarship applications, checking out the bulletin board or school website doesn't cut it. *You want the people who know about the money to know about you.* If they don't, how can they write compelling, winning recommendation letters on your behalf when you start applying for scholarships?

How much do your teachers, coaches, pastors, mentors, or employers really know about you? I'm not talking about your latest upload to YouTube or how many friends you have on MySpace. You need the people of influence in your academic life to know more about you.

You might be thinking, "Great, now The Scholarship Lady wants me to suck up to the teachers." I only want you to have the best chance at winning scholarships. A scholarship committee will *not* trust a letter of recommendation from your best friend or your grandma. It is so important to make a positive impression on the people who can influence your scholarship success.

A great way to break the ice is to ask these questions: "Did you go to college? Where did you go to college? Do you have any advice for me?" People will be dazzled and flattered that you exhibited interest, and they will remember you. Do not, *I repeat*, do not, at this stage walk up to these folks and say, "Can you help me find money for college?" It is insulting to ask them before you have built rapport. Ask them later, once you are on track with your dream and your plan and you have taken action and excelled in your efforts, which you will learn about throughout the book.

In junior year, grab a notebook and start jotting down all the activities, programs, and special recognition you've achieved in and out of school. This will help you build a base for finding scholarships related to your personal characteristics and accomplishments.

During junior year check out scholarship websites and create a profile for yourself. Some of the most successful sites are Scholarships.com and Fastweb.com; however, you can find dozens more on the Internet. The best scholarship websites do not charge a fee, and you should *not* pay anyone to provide this information. A good librarian can point you in the right direction if you or your parents want an old-fashioned printed listing.

Ask your counselor about students from your school who won scholarships last year. Write down the names of the scholarships and look at previous applications. If your school does not keep track of scholarship winners, maybe you can find names of winners in an old school newsletter or graduation program. Chat up the school librarian about the best scholarship listings for your area. Start collecting this information now so that when senior year hits you, fast and furious, you are one step ahead.

HOT TIP

Junior year is not too early to start looking for scholarships. Use time as your secret weapon in scoping out the scholarship possibilities long before your competition does!

101

Twelfth Grade/Senior Year

This is it. You apply to college during your senior year. Your competition is unbelievable. The number of students in your generation has created the highest college enrollment in the history of America. If you are confused, overwhelmed, and a little bit scared—don't panic. You *will* go to college. Also remember that *if you have more money you will have more choices*. Without cash for college you will probably end up with a mixture of grants, loans, and scholarships depending on many factors, including your family's income level. Although you cannot control how much money your parents make or whether your grandparents left you a trust fund, you *can* control how well you do in school and how well you apply for scholarships.

The Classified Ads

Wanted: Student Investors

Salary: $100 an Hour

Duties: Filling out Scholarship Applications

How can you earn $100 an hour? Look at it this way: If you invest five hours gathering information, writing a short essay, and sending it off to a scholarship judge—and you win a $500 scholarship, then you just earned $100 an hour!

You should know that much of the information requested on your *college* applications is actually based on your junior year. Good thing you were on track, right? Your senior-year grades and achievements are more noticeable on *scholarship* applications because the majority of applications are due in the spring of your senior year. To make your application shine, just keep up the good work (or kick it into high gear if necessary).

If your school offers advanced classes, enroll. If your school offers dual-enrollment, Advanced Placement (AP), or college courses, take them. Once you get to college and pay full tuition for every class, you will regret it if you did not use these low-or no-cost resources that can translate into college credit.

These challenging courses might require you to seek tutoring because they will be more rigorous than standard courses. Do not be intimidated or embarrassed to seek help. Just like success in algebra, success in AP courses is a positive indicator of college enrollment. You will be surrounded by other students who share your goals. If your friends aren't going to college and they hassle you, just remind them that unless they can help you pay for college, you have to take time to do your best in these classes.

What else should you do? Did you take the officer position with your school's Distributive Education Clubs of America (DECA) chapter? Did you enter any contests and win awards? Time is running out, and in addition to studying, going to basketball games, shopping at the mall, cleaning your room, working part-time, and babysitting your little brother, you need to make time to ensure that you will stand out on your scholarship applications. Please do not misinterpret "standing out" as advice to become an overachiever. Overachievers eventually burn out. Your best strategy is to focus and excel at what you do.

Invest in yourself or no one else will. You do not have to be a straight-A student to go to college or to win scholarships, but you do have to prove that you've done the best that you can. Life happens and scholarship judges understand that. Maybe you moved to America in seventh grade and your English isn't perfect. Maybe you have a recently diagnosed learning disability. Maybe you got in with the wrong crowd. It happens. *What matters is that you improve your situation.*

I know of one student who missed school due to brain surgery. His grades significantly declined. Over the years, he brought his grades back up, wrote a compelling essay for a scholarship application, and won the scholarship. This is an extreme example and I hope you don't have any serious illnesses that jeopardize your health, but you can tell that education was very important to this student and he turned his grades around.

Another student whom I advised was very average—too average. He just couldn't find a scholarship. He didn't do anything to make himself stand out, and his only hobby was playing video games. He couldn't articulate any passion for a possible major and wasn't engaged in school activities. I don't know if he ever won a scholarship, but I do know that he didn't invest in making himself the best that he could be—at least not in the scholarship world. Repeat with me: Invest in yourself or no one else will.

Team of Champions™

Another step toward scholarship success is building relationships. By now, you have built rapport with a few teachers, counselors, coaches, or mentors, right? It is time to form your Team of Champions. Team of what? Yes, champions. Let me share a quick lesson in why you need champions who will advocate for you.

ONE MENTOR. THREE STUDENTS. AND $17,500 IN SCHOLARSHIPS.

You might catch a glimpse of Patricia Torres Najera, if you can keep up with her. This mother of four who works full-time and volunteers with civic organizations is a trusted source to families who are puzzled about the transition to college.

In the past year, Patricia assisted three students in securing $17,500 in scholarships. These students were *not* her lifelong friends, or cousins, or neighbors, but Patricia saw the tremendous potential of these students and decided to help.

Patricia embodies the sprit of the *Scholarships 101* kitchen-table classroom, and she exemplifies the kind of person you want on your Team of Champions. She's not an official mentor, and there are no headquarters or special office. She looks for scholarships regularly, even though her own children are not in college yet. She passes good leads on to her network of family, friends, and co-workers. She does all of this in her spare time. Sounds like a hobby, doesn't it?

According to Patricia, she can best help students when she knows about their academic lives, personal lives, and family histories. Then, she can talk about the technical side of scholarships.

In one example, Patricia met a student who was surrounded by other people who were making bad choices inside and outside of school. For this young man, finishing high school and staying out of trouble was an enormous accomplishment. He had his mother and grandparents as a support system—until Patricia joined them. She became a champion for this student. Once she learned about his past and his prospects for a brighter future, she agreed to help him—if he agreed to do the hard work. Patricia taught him about scholarship applications, gave him firm deadlines, and helped him complete the Free Application for Federal Student Aid (FAFSA). The result was a financial aid package including scholarships that provided full-tuition support, a book allowance, and on-campus housing. This young man is the first in his family to attend college.

People such as Patricia are out there—you just need to find them. Look at mentoring programs in your city or try the old-fashioned approach of asking someone you know and respect.

Imagine with me that members of your local Rotary Club are offering scholarships and they are accepting applications from your school. Here are two common scenarios.

Nominations

In the first scenario, the Rotary Club called your principal and asked him or her to nominate five students to apply for one available scholarship. If the principal can only pick five students, he or she will probably ask the guidance counselors or department heads to forward names of students based on the criteria. If these decision makers don't know you, how can they forward your name? If they do know you and they forward your name, they can also put in a good word for you and boom—your name is on the list.

Promotion

In the second scenario, the Rotary Club bypasses the guidance department and runs an advertisement in the local paper requesting that students apply. Your grandma reads the paper, shows it to you, and says, "Honey, you are so smart, you should apply for this." You see that the application deadline is next week and it requires two letters of recommendation. Whom can you persuade to crank out a compelling letter in under a week? Your Team of Champions! These are people who care about you and want to see you succeed. Maybe they were the first in their families to go to college, just like you, and that is what motivates them to help. Maybe one was your Little League coach and he or she always hoped you would go to college someday. Your Team of Champions knows that you are worth the time. You have the grades but not the money, and they want to help you. Make a list of these people.

Team of Champions Exercise

Students: Make a list of everyone who could be a champion for your college-bound efforts. Include people in your family and outside of your family. Do people cheer you on and help you out? Are they quietly supporting your decision? This list should go beyond home and school and include your place of worship, work, and neighborhood. *Keep this list* as you read the book and start to think about everyone's role in your quest for college and scholarship money. You'll come back to this list throughout the book.

Your Future

If you want to attend college, you should consider it a long-term investment. Very few families can pay cash for college, especially because college tuition continues to rise faster than inflation and faster than the cost of health insurance. More students must work while they are in college, out of necessity, and more students are relying on student loans to pay for college.

The most important step in finding money for college is to complete the Free Application for Federal Student Aid, otherwise known as the FAFSA. The FAFSA is the common form that the U.S. Department of Education requires from students to determine eligibility for student aid, including grants and loans. Whether you apply for twenty scholarships or just one, *I strongly urge you to complete the FAFSA.*

FREE Help with the FAFSA!

Have you chewed your fingernails to the nub from worrying about the FAFSA? Stop chewing and check out College Goal Sunday. This free event is designed to assist college-bound students and their families, step-by-step, with completing the FAFSA. College financial aid administrators and other volunteers donate their expertise for your benefit. The National Association of Student Financial Aid Administrators (NASFAA), a credible professional organization, manages the program.

College Goal Sunday is available in nearly every state, but mark your calendar because it only happens *once a year in February.* To see where and when you can attend, go to www.collegegoalsundayusa.org.

To determine your estimated family contribution (EFC), the U.S. Department of Education uses a complicated formula based on your family income and the cost of the colleges you select. The Department of Education will send you your EFC on a Student Aid Report (SAR). Your EFC does not account for the cost of living in your area. You know that a dollar in Idaho is not the same as a dollar in New York, but on the FAFSA it doesn't matter. Sorry for this depressing news. The good news is that you will soon be a success at securing scholarships.

If your parents don't understand the FAFSA or why they are required to provide detailed information, ask them to call your school counselor or the financial aid office at any of the colleges where you applied. You are a potential customer at these colleges and their financial aid administrators are the real experts. Direct your questions to them. But a word of warning: Discussing family income can be awkward for everyone, including you and your parents. You might think, "They make tons of money, why can't they foot the bill?" or "How do we survive on this?"

Scholarship providers know that the FAFSA is used to assess needs from the government's standpoint, but some providers may have their own methods or they may require students to submit a College Scholarship Service (CSS) Profile (a service offered by the College Board), which uses different methods to calculate need.

The Feds, the FAFSA, Colleges, and You

The results of your FAFSA are the basis for need-based aid including grants, loans, and work-study. The federal government will distribute your results to the colleges that you indicated when you complete the FAFSA. Colleges use your EFC in their financial aid allocations. Scholarship providers may also use it to gauge your level of need. Don't be alarmed by this. You should complete the FAFSA because it can lead to more money. I should warn you, though, it is about as much fun as doing taxes or a thousand sit-ups.

Money is distributed to qualified students on a first-come-first-served basis until funds are depleted. You should fill out the FAFSA as soon as possible after January 1 each calendar year. *I recommend doing this by March 1 because many colleges and state grant programs have an early deadline that is tied to your FAFSA results.* Your parents will need to complete their taxes early. Ask your school for assistance completing the FAFSA or visit www.fafsa.ed.gov for detailed information and deadlines. Carefully type the website address, because bogus sites are out there to confuse you.

Quick Terms

Estimated Family Contribution (EFC): The amount that the federal government believes your family should contribute to the cost of college, based on the information you provide and the FAFSA calculations.

Free Application for Federal Student Aid (FAFSA): The form you will complete to determine if you qualify for need-based aid. The results are used by colleges to determine your eligibility for various forms of financial aid; some scholarship programs use the results, too.

FAFSA Shock: Your family's reaction to the EFC.

Let's move ahead and dive into something you have a little more control over: your future. What is motivating you to go to college? Do you want to work on Wall Street or become a crime-scene investigator? Buy a house or a new car someday? Do you want to make your family proud of you? Be a role model for your little sister? Start your own business? Change the world? Your dreams for the future will not only motivate *you* but the *people around you*. In chapter 3 we will have fun "dreaming big" about your future.

Fridge Notes

Freshman Year

❑ Do your best, and if necessary prioritize core classes over electives or activities.

❑ Strive for a B or better in all classes.

Sophomore Year

❑ Focus on core classes to build a base for higher-level classes.

❑ Invest time in career exploration. Conduct career-interest surveys, talk with interesting professionals, and search career websites.

❑ Take test-preparation classes. Take sample or preliminary tests in your school library or online.

Junior Year

❑ Make careful course selections and do more than the minimum.

❑ Pursue side jobs, hobbies, and clubs.

❑ Take the ACT or SAT tests, which are used by several scholarship committees and colleges as a gauge of your aptitude for college.

❑ Seek leadership positions in your school for activities that you enjoy.

❑ Tell everyone you know that you want to go to college. Ask questions of people whom you admire about how they achieved their goals.

❑ Show that you are on the path to college by investing in yourself.

❑ Start looking for scholarships.

Senior Year: Students

❑ Apply to college and keep up your grades.

❑ Do more than the minimum.

❑ Excel at what you do.

❑ Build your Team of Champions.

❑ Use all the resources at your school.

❑ Fill out the FAFSA at www.fafsa.ed.gov and ask your parents to get their taxes done early. You can submit a FAFSA after January 1 of your senior year, but don't wait too long.

❑ Meet all deadlines and give other people time to respond to your requests for information.

❑ Apply the principles you learn in *Scholarships 101.*

Senior Year: Parents

❑ Plan to complete your taxes early this year.

❑ Sign necessary forms, permission slips, and college materials as soon as possible.

❑ In the college-funding game, early is better and deadlines matter.

❑ If your child uses online college applications or the online FAFSA form, be sure to double-check spelling, dates, and details before pushing the "send" button.

Follow Your Dreams, and Others Will Too!

W e need more heroes. Not the spandex-wearing, flying-through-the-air kind, but the grew-up-on-a-farm-in-Kansas-went-to-college-and-eventually-became-Secretary-of-Agriculture kind, or the lived-in-the-Bronx-went-to-engineering-school-and-invented-a-better-lightbulb kind. We need people like you to go to college and pursue your dreams. I have spent nearly fifteen years helping students achieve their educational dreams, and now it's your turn.

You need to have a dream that you can share with other people so that they can support you. Even if you think you have a plan or a goal, do not skip this step, because dreaming is different. You don't settle in a dream. It's bigger and more colorful than a goal. If you want other people to help you, they need to buy into your dream. Scholarship judges, teachers, mentors, counselors, family members, coaches, and neighbors who can help you need to believe in you. I've seen passionless recommendation letters written for students, and I've seen those that are oozing joy. You can't pay someone to write a good letter of recommendation for you, so you need to provide something else—what they call in marketing the "warm fuzzies." This is how people feel when they see a puppy or do a good deed. You want people to feel good when they help you. You want them to feel proud of you through osmosis.

SCHOLARSHIPS FOR LUNCH

"I want a better future for my own family someday," Monica said softly. Monica sees how hard her mother works cleaning for businesses, and since her father passed away, life isn't easy. She currently helps her mom clean but doesn't want to do that forever, according to Monica. Monica and her brother are the first people in the history of their family to enroll in college.

Monica is currently attending a two-year college with plans to transfer to a four-year college to study physical therapy. "I love to work with children. It's inspiring. Disabled children don't necessarily know they have a disability."

To reach her goal of going to college, she realized she would need money because working part-time would not be enough. Her first stop was to meet face-to-face with her guidance counselor and ask other people for help. She approached two of her teachers and a friend who was already in college. Her mother only speaks Spanish, but Monica said, "My mom helped me with encouragement even though she couldn't help me with the applications."

Her teachers, counselor, and friend offered their help because they really wanted to see Monica go to college. They showed her applications and websites she could use and helped proofread her work.

"Start early so you can apply for more and win more," is Monica's advice for scholarship seekers. Although she checked out the national websites and applied for a few of the scholarships listed there, her gold mine was in local scholarships.

With activities such as soccer, DECA, and a church youth group, Monica had more than just academics going for her. She applied for, and won, four local scholarships totaling more than $3,000.

Her key to success? "During lunch hour, instead of going to lunch, I went to work on scholarships." Her best advice? "Work toward your dream—just keep doing it."

Document Your Dream

Your first step will be writing a short letter to someone you love or admire to tell him or her about your dream for the future. This is different from a career plan, which you may have done in high school. It is different from choosing a college. Your dream is necessarily big.

Use the dream-letter starter or use your own paper to write a letter to someone. Here are a few questions to answer as you write the letter:

1. Whom do you admire? Who will be most proud of you when you graduate from college? *You will address the letter to that person* (Dear Mom, Dear Dad, Dear Grandma, Dear Coach, etc.).

2. Next, you will tell the person your dream. Be descriptive. Why do you want to go to college? What are your reasons? What will you achieve? What are you willing to do?

3. To whom will you be held accountable? Use phrases such as "I want to go to college because . . ." or "I am willing to . . ." or "I promise you that . . ."

Dream Letter Starter

Use this template to get started on your dream letter. Your dream should be big.

Dear (fill in the blank),

I want to go to college because (fill in the blank).

My dream is (fill in the blank).

I promise you that (fill in the blank).

I will (fill in the blank), and (fill in the blank).

If ever I sound like I'm ready to give up, please (fill in the blank).

Thank you!

Love,

(your name)

The first part of the letter is very "dreamy," and you might feel corny or even emotional. When I've asked students to do this exercise in my workshops, some have fun with it and others treat it with deep respect. Students usually applaud when they hear one another's dreams. Because you are doing this alone, you might want to read your dream aloud or share the letter with the person to whom you addressed it. If you are a shy student, you might start by writing the letter to yourself as a personal promise.

You will immediately increase your likelihood of success if you add action to your dream. Try adding specific goals. Notice the difference in these two letters.

Letter #1 to Grandma

Dear Grandma,

I want to go to college to make you proud, and I promise to get good grades and work hard. It's my dream to buy you a house someday. I know you love me and I love you too, and I won't let you down . . .

Beautiful dream. Now let's add some key accomplishment phrases to make it more specific.

Letter #2 to Grandma

Dear Grandma,

I want to go to college to become a teacher just like you. My dream is to work back in the old neighborhood so kids can see that they can make it, too. I promise you that I will enroll in a four-year college in the fall and I will keep my GPA above a 3.0. I will show you my grades each semester and I will graduate from college. I will apply for financial aid and I will apply for five scholarships this month. I know you love me and I love you too. If I need help, I will ask for it, but if you can tell I'm struggling, would you send me some of your chocolate chip cookies when I'm in college? I won't let you down. You have my word.

Do you see the difference?

Right now you might be thinking, "The Scholarship Lady is nuts," or, "This is childish, I'm not doing this." Trust me. I know that if you are motivated and able to articulate your dream and your goals to other people, you will be legions ahead of your competition. I have heard several versions of "Letter #1 to Grandma" in my scholarship workshops, and it is a fine letter for your grandma. What I've learned, however, is that kind of dream doesn't set you apart from other students. Everyone who is reading this book wants to go to college and win scholarships and make someone proud. Your dream needs to be more specific to hold yourself accountable. How do you define "get good grades?" If you go to college, will you graduate? You will if you are committed and think you will. In case you are not aware, most people who enroll in college do *not* earn degrees within four years and only about two-thirds graduate within six years. By adding actions to your dream, you will immediately strive for results that are higher than other students'.

Let's look at the second letter. It shows that you have specific, realistic objectives with deadlines. This will contribute to your goal of going to college, becoming a teacher, and working in your old neighborhood. Other students say, "I'm going to college." You say, "I'm going to college and will earn a degree."

Next, recraft your letter for a broader audience if necessary. You might want to leave out very personal details if you included any. The first letter might be very personal, and you should keep it when you need that extra kick of motivation, but you want to have a version that you can share with a broader audience, too. Think of it as your pitch or your personal statement. Colleges ask for personal statements as part of the application process. Revise it for this exercise, if you like.

Once you have a version of your dream that you are comfortable sharing with someone such as a teacher, counselor, or member of your Team of Champions, read it aloud. Why? If you say the words and hear them, it becomes more real. In the future you will share your dream, or a condensed version of your dream, with others and it needs to sound sincere. If you don't believe in your dream, it will be hard to convince others. Excerpts from your dream letter may become part of your scholarship essays or college applications. Keep finessing it until it sounds just right.

You don't want to *sound* like a dreamer, though. You want to sound like a *dreamer with a plan*. Remember, scholarship judges are professionals who want to make good investments.

Motivational Mantras

"What do you pack to pursue a dream, and what do you leave behind?" That's a quote from Sandra Sharpe, and it is on my desk, along with an old postcard from my friend Marjorie that says simply, "You Go Girl." These two daily mantras help motivate me, and they greet me every time I sit down at my computer. What's your favorite quote or motto? Is it related to your goals and dreams?

If you want to go to college and accumulate scholarship money, you will be required to make sacrifices. You must carefully decide how you spend your time.

You need to put your dream in front of you every day. Write it down. Put it in your locker, on your mirror, above the coat rack, or on your fridge. Look at it everyday. Are you working toward your dream?

BOOST YOURSELF AND OTHERS WILL HELP

Karlton built his Team of Champions by networking and sharing his dream with key people. "Book work is important, but you have to be connected to elevate yourself to the better opportunities," he said.

Karlton's scholarship-winning résumé sounds similar to other students': National Honor Society, track, cross-country, volunteering, and yearbook. As a student at a large, public school he realized that if he wanted to compete for scholarships, he had to find other ways to stand out.

He relied on a Team of Champions that included his guidance counselor, cousin, grandmother, precollege advisor, and admissions counselor to help him pursue his goal of majoring in architecture and securing scholarships to enroll. It was his cousin who alerted him to a new, local, summer program for aspiring architects. Karlton earned a scholarship to attend in the summer between his junior and senior year. This was in addition to another summer precollege program that he already attended.

The summer experience solidified his goals for pursuing the major, and while participating, he impressed the admissions counselor in the school of architecture. In the long run, this paid off. After applying and gaining acceptance to that college, the school offered him a $5,000 scholarship. His relationship with the admissions counselor is still important because he is personally alerted when more scholarships are being offered. These kinds of opportunities don't "just happen," according to Karlton. "Everything I did in high school was to boost myself higher," he said.

Of the fifteen scholarships Karlton applied for, he won seven—that's about half of them! Karlton said he wrote one permanent essay and made it the absolute best it could be. Then he changed it a little bit depending on the specific scholarship essay question. "My grandma kept on me about the deadlines and she helped proofread my essays."

What's his best scholarship advice? "Have a network of people and start early."

Achieve Your Dream

Other people want you to succeed, but you may not even know them yet. If you are already surrounded by positive people who are cheering you on, you are incredibly lucky and should count your blessings! If you are surrounded by people who bring you down, put you down, or tell you that you'll never make it, then you need to convince them otherwise or find new people to surround you. You want to surround yourself with people who believe in you and people who have their own goals. Remember: Most people who apply for scholarships do *not* win them. You want to be in the group that *does* win, and that requires you to be associated with successful people who can become a member of your Team of Champions.

One part of my business is assisting precollege programs with evaluating student programs. As part of the evaluations, we ask students to complete surveys about their college-bound experiences. I am amazed when we ask the question, "Has anyone tried to prevent you from going to college?" and students answer "yes." When we ask, "Who?" the answers have been friends and sometimes parents. This is shocking but true. Sometimes your friends or even your parents don't want you to think "you're all that," or they are afraid what will happen to you, or to them, if you leave. These are very real thoughts and fears for a small number of students. Perhaps you grew up in a very small community and your loved ones are afraid of you attending college in a big city. Maybe you are part of close-knit religious group that is fearful of temptation turning you into a morally deficient college student. Perhaps your friends aren't going anywhere in life and they are freaking out about who they will hang with if you're gone. These people may knowingly or unknowingly sabotage your efforts. It is rare but real. Be prepared to stay strong and keep your focus if someone tries to dissuade you.

Back to achieving your dream.

In the book *The Pact*, three doctors who were raised in Newark, New Jersey, tell their compelling story of how they stuck together and promised one another they would become doctors—and they did. Look around you. Who else shares the same ideals that you have about a prosperous future? If you don't see other students or you aren't sure, then be the leader and ask people to join you in your quest. If you have great friends who are all going to college, and your parents went to college, your path might be a little easier.

Two main barriers prevent students from attending college: (1) financial barriers, and (2) academic preparedness. Assuming that you are academically prepared, plan to go to college, and have a dream (a lot of assumptions here), you need to invest a considerable amount of time in finding money for college. Very rarely does a scholarship sponsor come looking for you. Are you willing to invest time in the quest for scholarships? Most students think the first step is searching the Internet for scholarships. Wrong. You know that *investing in yourself* is the first step. Next, build your Team of Champions. Then, articulate your dream and broaden your circle of supporters.

Bull's Eye

Several people and organizations will play a role in your quest for scholarships. Look around you. Think in concentric circles, such as a dartboard, with you in the bull's eye. You're on a hunt for resources and you're going to start in your family. Who else in your family went to college? Did they win scholarships? How about your friends? Are they already in college? Expand the circle and look at your school.

Who in your school is the information gatekeeper for college information? Is it the secretary, guidance counselor, senior advisor, or someone else? Find out who. Figure 3–1 illustrates what I am talking about.

Figure 3–1. Your circles of resources.

In the next circle, look at businesses in your community. Find out if the chamber of commerce in your town offers scholarships or maintains a list of those who do. What about local stores? Maybe your grocery store is a member of a national grocers' organization that nominates one student for a scholarship each year. Large department stores oftentimes have scholarships. Target and Kohl's, two of America's largest retailers, both offer scholarships.

Do nearby colleges offer "precollege" or summer programs for high school students? Are you enrolled? Do they offer financial aid clinics to the public? Whether you plan to attend a particular college or not, you can probably attend its public workshops for free. Have you ever visited a college campus before? If you have not, plan to do so soon! If you don't have a formal college tour planned, visit the college nearest your home. Call ahead and find out when it offers tours, or go with a group of friends to explore. This experience is worth every penny.

When you are visiting a college, cruise through the financial aid office and review its scholarship listings. They are usually posted on a bulletin board or on a website, but that is a small sampling of all the scholarships offered.

Your local library is a great place to gather information, but it can be overwhelming if you live in a large city with a mammoth library. Be clear and be focused so you don't get distracted. Libraries stock books on scholarships and they may have fast Internet access, but they are also repositories for community postings and announcements. When scholarship providers want to spread the word, they will often send fliers to the libraries. In smaller towns, this is especially true. If you haven't been to a library in a while, now is the time to go. Librarians are information experts and they can point you in the right direction, which beats wandering around by yourself. If your library staffs a young adult librarian, get to know this person. He or she can alert you when special events are scheduled or new materials are coming in, and this person may have special young-adult programs. If you're feeling like a social entrepreneur, post your own sign to create a scholarship club or college club.

Reconnect with positive places that influenced you growing up. Imagine the face of an old coach, youth mentor, or 4-H club leader. Were you a regular at the Boys & Girls Club? Even if the same staff members don't work there, the organizations really want to see and hear from alumni. Believe me, I've had the task of tracking down former students in education programs, and I always love hearing from them. Whether they had good news or bad news to share, I still wanted to hear about it. Remember, you are building a road map of people and places that can help you find scholarships or connect you to other resources for colleges. You want to share your dream with the people who know about the resources. These youth-focused organizations could be members of larger networks or associations, and they may award scholarships to current and former participants.

So, what are you going to say to these people who may or may not know you? Try translating your dream (which inspires you and those around you) into a thirty-second summary. This is sometimes called your elevator speech or elevator pitch. In other words, what would you say to someone if you only had thirty seconds? Also, work on your introduction. How you greet people says a lot about you. Look people in the eye and be sincere. Ask for advice, don't demand it. Try to make a connection. Be yourself. If you know the people, it's much easier to do this. If you don't know them, remember, you are just asking for a little help. Here are a few scenarios of how this might go down.

Scenario #1

You go back to the Boys & Girls Club where you hung out as a kid and you stop at the front desk.

> **You:** "Hey, what's up?"
>
> **Them:** "Not much."
>
> **You:** "I used to come here after school when I was little. My name is James. Does Dionne still work here? He was my favorite coach."
>
> **Them:** "No, Dionne's been gone awhile."
>
> **You:** "Well, I wanted to stop in and let him know that I'm going to college to become a teacher."
>
> **Them:** "That's cool. Where do you go to school now?"
>
> **You:** "I'm a senior at McArthur High. I'm trying to find scholarships to go to Florida State in the fall. Does the Boys & Girls Club have any scholarships?"

The person may say yes or no about the scholarships, or he or she might keep up the chitchat or ask you more questions. The point is you have reintroduced yourself to an organization that would be wise to connect with your success. You might consider volunteering there or ask if you can talk to the younger kids about staying in school. The possibilities are endless. Last, leave your phone number with the front desk or ask if there is an education director or education coordinator who can alert you about any scholarships. You need to plant the seed. If the person is interested in you or if your old coach is still there, go ahead and share your dream.

Scenario #2

You stop in the public library, which you haven't done in years because you use your school library or the Internet to do research. You approach a librarian.

> **You:** "Excuse me please. Can you tell me where you keep your collection of college information? I'm looking for scholarships to start school in the fall." (This is a very common request at libraries.)
>
> **Librarian:** "Sure, the books are over there on that wall."
>
> **You:** "Okay, thank you. In addition to the books, do you have any special events or college-planning sessions here at the library?"
>
> **Librarian:** "No, we don't really do that, but sometimes we get mail from the colleges."
>
> **You:** "I want to collect as many resources as possible. Do you have any other suggestions?"

The point at the library is to ask information-seeking questions. They probably don't know you personally, but if you start to hang out there and show that you are serious about finding scholarships, the staff will take notice. When I managed a mobile college-advising program, libraries hosted our workers during after-school and weekend hours. What I noticed is that students who stopped in once for quick advice yielded what they invested— little. Students who sought resources seriously yielded much more. In a library, expect staff members to point you to the resources, but don't expect them to hang out with you and find scholarships. It is possible, however, that if they get to know you, they'll keep a lookout for materials and keep you informed about the latest resources.

Scenario #3

You visit the stables where you rode horses last summer. You approach the barn manager.

> **You:** "Hey, Jack, it's me, Sophia, from last year."
>
> **Jack:** "Sophia, how's it going? We haven't seen you out here since last summer. What have you been doing?"

You: "Well, I've been studying a lot and getting ready to go to college. I want to be a veterinarian."

Jack: "That is just great. How are your folks?"

You: "They're doing great. We're all just a little nervous about paying for college. You know I really loved coming here and I want to become a vet someday. It's really my dream to open a new animal hospital in Reedsburg."

Jack: "That's pretty impressive."

You: "I have a 3.2 GPA and I got accepted at three colleges. I just need to focus on scholarships now. I was wondering if you know of any scholarships for people like me."

Jack: "Well, I'm not sure, but I think the Equestrian Society started a scholarship a few years ago. I can check for you if you like."

You: "That would be so great. I'll leave my number up at the office. Any help or connections you can make would really help us out."

Jack: "No problem. You know what, I have the number of a vet we use. Maybe she would be willing to talk with you, too."

The point of this scenario is that if you meet people who know you or remember you, make sure to share your dream! You have no idea how many people will be proud to support you and may try to live vicariously through you. If you are shy, you might struggle the first few times that you ask people for help, but keep practicing!

If you have a favorite teacher, make sure you tell him or her your dream. Teachers' unions and teachers' associations also have scholarships. Ask a teacher: "How did you become a teacher?" The teacher might be willing to share his or her story.

Look at your life. Think about these questions:

■ Where have you been and where do you want to go?

■ What do you need to do to achieve your dream?

■ Who can help you get there?

■ Who is connected to the resources you need?

Whose Dream Is It?

I have met students who tell me that they dream of becoming doctors, but their actions undermine their dreams. They miss deadlines. They don't enroll in premed studies. They are scraping by with a B-minus in biology. Not the kind of doctor I would want. I am immediately suspect of their dreams and I ask them, "Whose dream is it?"

The reality is often that one of the student's parents was a doctor or someone else wants the student to become a doctor, so the student feels like he or she must fulfill a legacy. The pressure can seem insurmountable, especially if the student feels a duty to honor those wishes. This breaks my heart.

You need to remind yourself, and remind others, respectfully, of course, that you will be more successful if you follow your own dream. This is what will motivate you and provide that personal push when you complete your scholarship applications. Many scholarships are given to aspiring professionals in a chosen field, but if you really don't want to be a doctor, pharmacist, teacher, lawyer, or whatever it is, you will exude less passion than a person who really wants it. It's hard to fake passion unless you are a really good actor. In which case, acting may be your calling!

The Guidance Office:
One Step on the Yellow Brick Road

The road to college scholarships includes many stops, as is shown in figure 3-2. Your first stop should be the guidance office at your school, if the school has one.

The average counselor in a high school is assigned more than 300 students. At the schools I worked with, it was closer to 400 students per counselor. Traditionally, counselors focus on crisis situations, personal counseling, dropout prevention, psychological issues, and other problem solving. These folks are also required to handle scheduling, testing, and discipline on top of assisting you with the transition to life after high school. Some students avoid the counselors, so only the very high-achieving students or trouble-prone students often end up in the guidance office. What is the situation at your school?

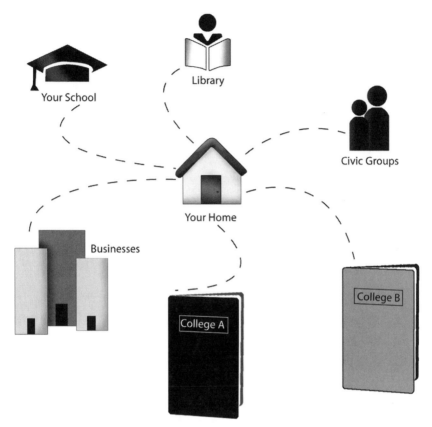

Figure 3–2. The scholarship road map.

If you have a counselor devoted to college admissions and financial aid, you are lucky. This is more prevalent at private, college-prep high schools or well-funded schools, and it is less prevalent in rural or heavily populated urban public schools. If you want the counseling staff's attention for something other than ditching class, you need to stand out in a positive way. I'm guessing if you are a college-bound student, you have lots of positive ways to stand out. As you begin to navigate the college and financial aid jungle, be pleasantly persistent with the adults in your school who can help you.

Yes, it is a counselor's job to provide you with information and advice about postsecondary planning, but it is your job to seek all of the resources that can help you achieve your goals. Students who win scholarships know their counselors but do not stop there when seeking scholarship information and support. The guidance office at your school is only one step on the road to scholarship success. Keep moving.

So what should you do with your dream? Add your plan! Not just any plan, but your personalized plan of how you are going to move from being a cash-strapped high school student into a scholarship-wielding force.

Chapter 4

College Prep

Your ability to win scholarships for college is closely tied to your investment in college preparation. Whether it's completing an ACT or SAT prep class or touring the eastern seaboard for campus visits, these activities make a difference in your Fabulous Factor™. Incredible resources already exist; you just need to find them.

Fabulous Factor

A student's Fabulous Factor is subjective. In my mind, it is determined by a combination of the student's past experiences, academic achievement, goals for the future, answers on the scholarship application, the essay, and the competition. You want a judge to read your application, review your materials, and think, "this student is fabulous!"

Successful students participate in precollege programs or engage in unique experiences to set themselves apart. To the parents who started enrolling their children in summer science classes in middle school, "just for fun," you know what I mean.

Traditional College-Prep Experiences

College-prep programs can expose students to new experiences and new places and help them build their skills. Whether it's a one-time Saturday workshop at a local college or a four-year program that provides everything from test prep to tutoring, you can improve your Fabulous Factor by enrolling in college-prep programs. What you need depends on your academic and personal background, your exposure to the college experience, and your level of preparedness for college. And, to some extent, your bank account. Precollege programs can range from no cost to low cost to a couple thousand bucks.

College-prep experiences can be formal or informal. Here are a few examples.

- **ACT or SAT Preparation Classes**. An ACT score of 22 might open the doors to a community college, but it's not Ivy League material. Even a score of 30, depending on your dream college, could be considered average. To boost your test scores you can take online or in-person test preparation, and if you are not happy with your score, you can retake the test. Large companies such as Sylvan or Kaplan also offer private or small-group tutoring. You can sign up for online classes and workshop-based learning and supplement that with books and manuals. They cost money, but your school district might provide assistance for the most basic test-prep classes in your area if you qualify for free or reduced-cost lunch. Ask about this if you think you might qualify. The relationship between test scores and scholarships varies greatly for private scholarships because every scholarship sponsor sets its own criteria. But it can't hurt to have a good score. If your college offers scholarships based on a minimum test score, the level of importance increases.

- **College Tours**. A multicity college tour is a right of passage in some families. Usually planned for late in the student's junior year, over the summer, or during fall of the student's senior year at the latest, these jaunts around the country help students and parents see the difference between what is printed in a brochure and what a campus really offers. They fly, drive, or otherwise embark on a journey to check out the possibilities. It's a road trip with a college-bound mission. The cost is a few tanks of gas, airline tickets, or your sanity if you and your travel companion differ on the concept of "the perfect college." Pack your patience *and* your headphones.

High schools, civic groups, and precollege programs may offer larger group tours over a region of the United States or to categories of colleges such as Ivy League schools, Big Ten universities, art colleges, or historically Black colleges. For students who have never left their hometowns, this sounds exciting, but it can be overwhelming. If you go on a trip like this, make sure you are mentally and emotionally prepared. As for scholarships, ask a question such as, "What scholarship opportunities do you offer for (fill in the blank) people like me, out-of-state students, engineering majors, etc.?" Leaders of large tour groups often can't go into great detail, but you should begin to get comfortable asking these kinds of questions. Your tour might include a stop at the financial aid office.

■ **College-Based Classes.** Are you fascinated by astronomy and biology? Math and music? Colleges offer a variety of experiences that are open to the public through special events or through program enrollment. In my town these classes are called "College for Teens" or "Kids on Campus." Depending on the university and the purpose of the course, the level of difficulty can range from two hours building toothpick bridges to spending a week on a research vessel analyzing water pollution. In more structured programs, you may be able to earn college credit. If you've never experienced a precollege class like this, I strongly recommend it. You may discover a new interest or realize a hidden talent you possess. Think of it as soccer camp for your brain.

After your experience, you can then put the activity on your scholarship résumé as further proof of your scholarship worthiness. These classes, much like the test-prep classes, can go from zero to a few thousand bucks depending on the nature of the course. Set a budget, even if it's fifty dollars, and try a class that sounds like fun.

■ **Precollege Programs.** Ranging from exclusive experiences that you can win through competition to local, supportive programs for first-generation college students, precollege programs are usually characterized by a higher level of commitment by the students who enroll and the professionals who manage the program. They can be two-week camps for future nurses or four-year-long comprehensive programs that provide mentoring, tutoring, financial aid workshops, college-application assistance, and organized college tours. The longer programs, starting in ninth grade, are often federally funded and target economically disadvantaged youth who would otherwise never have the opportunities mentioned above.

College Credit

Linking Learning to Life is a nonprofit organization in Vermont. It offers youth a variety of programs and services including mentoring, community-based learning, service learning, job shadowing, student internships, career exploration, employment, and postsecondary opportunities.

Linking Learning to Life manages College Connections, a program that offers Vermont tenth- through twelfth-graders options for exploring post-secondary education prior to graduation. To earn dual-enrollment credit and to experience real college-level classes, students can take college courses while still in high school. The benefit of dual enrollment is that upon successful completion, students earn both high school *and* college credit. Linking Learning to Life has arranged for low- or no-cost credits depending on family income.

Linking Learning to Life partners with Burlington College, Champlain College, Community College of Vermont, Saint Michael's College, the University of Vermont, and Vermont Technical College to make this possible.

Although College Connections is open to all students, it is particularly designed to benefit students who may not see themselves as college-bound for a variety of reasons. The College Connections coordinator provides information to school administrators, guidance staff, special educators, classroom teachers, and to parents of prospective students.

College Connections is developing ways to support students once they have gone on to college. Several college partners initiated these "college success" strategies with the goal of helping students successfully earn degrees.

Look for these types of programs in your area. To learn more about College Connections in Vermont, check out www.linkinglearningto life.org.

Summertime is the perfect time to try any of these experiences. Colleges are the most likely source to offer these programs, but local organizations sometimes serve as sponsors. The easiest way to find one is to ask in your guidance department or type "precollege" or "college preparation" into an Internet search engine. If you are limited by how far you can travel, add the name of your city, county, or state to the search terms. You might also visit the websites of colleges in your area and keyword search there.

Alternative College-Prep Experiences

What should you do if your parents can't afford these college-prep experiences? I see four choices: (1) find a program designed for lower-income students, (2) raise money to pay the enrollment fees, (3) find free or very low-cost events, or (4) create your own experience. Here's how.

1. **Find Low-Income Student Programs.** Programs for low-income or first-generation students are operated by community foundations, colleges, state and federal governments, nonprofit groups, and similar organizations. The U.S. Department of Education funds several programs around the country called TRIO, GEAR UP, Upward Bound, and Talent Search. A list of more than 800 public and private programs can be found through the National College Access Network or the Pathways to College Network. Visit the www.scholarshipstreet.com resource page for direct links to both of these organizations or go directly to http://www.collegeaccess.org or http://www.pathwaystocollege.net.

Wow! $2.8 Million in Scholarships!

If you live in Cleveland, you are neighbors with one of the oldest, largest, most helpful scholarship and advising programs in the country.

Cleveland Scholarship Programs, Inc. (CSP) inspires and motivates people to achieve their full potential through education. CSP partners with schools, and starting in sixth grade, provides workshops and individual advising on college awareness, college readiness, career awareness, financial aid, and other services.

In the 2006–2007 school year, CSP awarded nearly $3 million in scholarships to more than two thousand students. Participating students value CSP not only for the scholarships but for the incredible support of the staff. CSP scholarships are called "last-dollar scholarships" and are designed to meet the unmet need, or gap, that some students experience when they enroll in college. CSP also follows up with participating students over the summer and into college to make sure students succeed once they arrive on campus. Although the majority of CSP scholarships target disadvantaged students, they also manage scholarships for other organizations that may or may not use family income as criteria for their scholarships.

Whether you are enrolled in a CSP program or not, you can still find expert advice on college and financial aid issues by visiting the CSP Resource Center in downtown Cleveland. The resource center is open to the public, for free, six days a week.

If you live in the Cleveland area or northeast Ohio, make sure you check out CSP! Start here: www.cspohio.org.

---

2. **Raise Money**. Raise money for the program by asking for pledges, doing chores, working part-time, or selling something you don't need. I know that it's rare to find a student who is going to use his or her spare money to enroll in a college program, but think about your Team of Champions. Is there some way the team could "sponsor" you? Can you mow lawns? Babysit? Parents, can you plan a rummage sale or go on a

financial diet for one week? Pack lunch instead of eating out? Ask about scholarships at the program, too. Many of the precollege courses offer income-based or achievement-based scholarships.

3. **Go to Free Events**. Find free or low-cost events offered by community groups, colleges, and libraries. I strongly recommend attending free concerts, lectures, and open houses at local colleges. You can also schedule free campus visits on your own. Sometimes they are boring and sometimes they are over-the-top. The point is to visit a college campus if you have never done so. Sure, the college is trying to recruit you, but you can soak it in and get a feel for the campus. One of my favorite events is an open house my alma mater holds every October. It is a party with free food, musical performances, science experiments, guest speakers, team mascots, student groups, and much more. It meets the truest definition of *extravaganza*. It also promotes the school's precollege programs, and you can ask people about scholarships in a low-pressure environment. Bonus: Everyone hands out free Halloween candy!

4. **Make Your Own**. Create your own precollege experience. If you can't afford a long trip, try carpooling with another family to colleges in your state, and split the cost of fuel. You could form your own college club, either officially (which would look good on your scholarship applications!) by asking a teacher to be your advisor, or unofficially by meeting with a group of friends once a week. The benefit of having an official club is that you might be able to do fund-raising to pay for some precollege classes. What can you do in these groups? Compare colleges, search for scholarships, proofread one another's essays, study for placement tests, or simply encourage one another. It's free and you'll be with people you like, right?

If my passion for precollege programs hasn't hit you yet, I have a confession to make: I created a precollege program, I conduct research for precollege programs, and I am a guest speaker for precollege programs. "Scholarship Boot Camp," "Scholarship Success," "Show Me the Money," and "Life After High School" are just a few titles. Through my research on other precollege programs, I know that students who participate value the experience highly, they gain skills that give them an edge, they meet other college-bound students, and most important, they have fun learning. When's the last time you had fun learning? I hope it was recently. If not, check out a precollege class or program.

Let's take a look at how some of these programs can directly affect your scholarship success.

■ **Scenario 1: An Open House at a College.** You and your friends decide to check out a local college. You mom decides to go along, too. Hey, at least you have a ride home. When you arrive in the student union (a place on campus where people gather) you are greeted by students who hand you a brochure about every single exhibit, booth, and performance that day. You decide to visit the "anthropology lab" first, where people have constructed a pseudo dorm room so visitors can study the subculture of dorm dwellers—just for fun. As you begin talking with a representative from the Anthropology department, you learn that she just received a major grant to increase her research in Central America. There will be new positions for research assistants and a few scholarships for undergraduates.

How would you learn out about this if you didn't attend the open house? In the newspaper? Probably not. You are very interested in this college and are considering anthropology as a major. The representative asks you to fill out an interest form, gives you a free notepad, and hands you her card. You have just made one connection to a possible scholarship. Granted, she's probably doing the same thing with every student who stops at her booth, but at least you know a name and a face, should you choose this college.

■ **Scenario 2: A Weekend Class During the Spring at a Local College.** As you're walking to class, you notice a new poster on the wall: "Future Teachers Weekend—Sign Up Now!" A local college and an organization of retired teachers hosts the free event every year for twenty students. The word *free* catches your eye, so you submit a one-page application even though you're not sure that you want to go to that college. A few weeks later, you get an e-mail saying that you have been selected to participate in the program, which consists of an orientation on a Friday night and a day-long series of workshops on a Saturday. Great! You're in!

When you arrive at the orientation, you are very nervous and don't know anyone, but the first exercise is to interview someone else in the room. To be polite, you pick the gentleman sitting next to you. As you begin to ask him about who he is, what he does, etc., you learn that he graduated from your high school more than thirty years ago and his grandson goes to your school. He has helped organize the event and he is the president of the retired teachers' association. The association offers a scholarship. Lucky you. You make a note to follow up on this over the weekend.

During the Future Teachers' Weekend, you hear from current students who talk about student teaching, the dean of students in the School of Education discusses the school's academic plan, and two current teachers tell you about the joys and stresses of teaching. You attend a workshop on how lesson plans are created and another one on writing an essay about why you want to become a teacher. Your lunchtime speaker lays out the "Top Ten Reasons to Choose Teaching as a Career." This is hard work and you are on the verge of information overload.

Then you attend one more session, titled "How to Pay for College." You learn that if you agree to stay in the state after graduation, you can get part of your tuition paid for, and if you agree to teach in a rural or urban area, you can receive money to help pay off your student loans. Suddenly, you're not so tired. Free money to become a teacher? Yes. You don't believe it, so you ask the nice gentlemen you interviewed earlier and he confirms it's true. Whether you choose this college or not, it's good to know the money is out there.

At the closing reception, the woman in charge of the event announces that the organization will accept applications from the students who attended the weekend class for a week-long on-campus program during the summer. The college is sponsoring the summer program and it will only select five students from your group because other departments are also participating and will select their own students. The cost is $495. However, she tells you that students will have a once-in-a-lifetime opportunity and that a few scholarships are available from the retired teachers' association. Definitely worth pursuing! You have learned about a college scholarship from a retired teacher, state and national scholarship programs that will reimburse you after you graduate, and a scholarship to help you pay for the week-long summer camp for teachers. It's a three pointer! Luis Quiñones, pictured on page 52, worked with many people, including a precollege advisor at his school, to learn about scholarships and won a scholarship from the Wisconsin Education Association of Student Support Programs (WEASSP).

■ **Scenario 3: College Competition for High School Students.** Hanging out at the beach can offer more than surf, sand, and sun, and your biology teacher knows this. For the last three years your school has participated in the National Ocean

Luis Quiñones.

Sciences Bowl (NOSB), and this year one of your friends asks you to join the team. You're not sure that you're ready to trade in your surfboard for a microscope, but you do love the ocean. The NOSB is an academic competition and if you win the regionals, you will advance to the nationals, which includes an all-expenses-paid trip to a college that is known for marine sciences. Through your participation in the bowl, you also become eligible for internships and college scholarships.

Your friend convinces you to join the team, and you suddenly see a lot more of your biology teacher, who is the coach for your team. Your team studies after school once a week and then you quiz yourself at home. This is a lot of work, but you get to learn more about the bay where you grew up and how it's changing over time. The prize this year sounds pretty cool, too—the winning team earns a free trip to a college in New York.

You are pretty good at math and science and you begin to learn a lot more specifically in biology, geology, and chemistry. The competition is held at a college, and this gives you a chance to meet professors and professionals who are experts in the field. You learn from one of the judges that this particular campus has a long history of giving scholarships to students like you. Let's recap here. You are already taking advanced biology; you just have to commit an extra hour per week to your team and the weekend quizzes. You get to hang out with your friend and other students whom you didn't know cared about the ocean just like you do. If you win, there's a free trip plus possible internships, and you can then apply for national scholarships; plus, your local college has scholarships, too. Where do I sign up?

You will notice in all of the examples that you had to do some extra work beyond what's required in your classes or what you need to graduate. You put yourself in a place with like-minded people and met students and professionals who share your interests. You also learned about scholarship opportunities even though that wasn't advertised in the program description.

If your family regularly socializes with marine biologists, teachers, professors, anthropologists, engineers, and nurses, then you are probably more familiar with these types of scholarship programs. When I was in high school, one of my uncles had a degree in architecture and my mom had a two-year degree in drafting. All of the other adults I knew in my family worked in factories or offices. If you, like me, had little exposure to college-educated professionals and the related college-preparation experiences I described, please find, enroll, or join a precollege program.

Fridge Notes

Ready for College

❑ Invest in test prep or tutoring if you need it.

❑ Visit college campuses in your county or state, for starters. Plan a road trip with another family to make it more fun.

❑ Investigate college-prep or precollege programs in your area. If your budget is flexible, look at national programs. What interests you? Can you ask a friend to go with you?

❑ Create a college-prep club if you do not attend a college-prep high school. Surround yourself with people who have similar goals.

❑ Think scholarships! In your conversations and your actions, let people know you are looking for scholarships.

❑ Add your new experiences to your scholarship worksheet and résumé.

❑ Think about these experiences. Were they fun? Boring? Exciting? Scary? Why? Use your answers to guide your next choice.

Behind the Scenes

Are you ready to impress a middle-aged administrator who is tired of reading bad scholarship essays? Do you understand how the scholarship process works behind the scenes?

Before you apply for any scholarships, it would be beneficial to understand how scholarship providers operate and what influences their decision-making process. Although this is a diverse group ranging from multi-million-dollar organizations to volunteer-run local associations, a few tenets are true.

Reality Check

Scholarship sponsors are a generous group of individuals and organizations. A 2005 report by the Institute for Higher Education Policy estimates that more than $3 billion a year is distributed in the United States in private scholarship dollars. This does not include money distributed through very small organizations or through tuition discounting or institutional-based giving at colleges.

Quick Terms

Institutional-Based Aid: Financial aid distributed from the colleges' own funds or grants they administer for another entity, such as a state agency.

Preferential Packaging: The practice of using institutional aid (scholarships and grants) to lure or recruit students to a college. Less emphasis is put on self-help aid.

Follow me on a journey into the world of scholarship administrators. You are going to see and hear everything going on in the days leading up to a scholarship deadline for a small association scholarship, a college-based freshman scholarship, and a major national scholarship. By the way, I've created dramatizations so I can make my point quickly and you can get the information you need.

Office #1, Local Chapter of the Lions Club

Sal Lewinsky drops his golf clubs in the corner of the office. As president of the Lions Club, he stops in a few times a week to answer messages, organize bingo night, and manage the scholarship fund. He presses the answering-machine button to listen to his messages (yes, he has an answering machine).

> **Caller #1:** "Hi. Ummm. I noticed your deadline is this Friday for your scholarship and I'm wondering if it's worth it for me to apply. Can you call me back . . . ?"
>
> **Caller #2:** "Good morning. My son attends Lincoln High School and even though his school isn't on your list, I'm wondering if you would make an exception because he meets all of the other criteria and could really use this scholarship. Can you call me back please . . ."
>
> **Caller #3:** "Hi. I'd like you to e-mail your application to me. The directions said to request a copy by mail but I know the deadline is coming soon. My e-mail is . . ."

Caller #4: "Good morning. I sent in my application last week and forgot to submit my letters of recommendation. I wanted to know your hours so I can drop those off by Friday, or could you give me your fax number? Please call me or e-mail me your hours . . ."

Caller #5: "Hey Sal, it's Lou Romantini. My nephew Jake applied for the scholarship and I just wanted to put in a good word for him. See you next month at the banquet."

Caller #6: "Hi Mr. Lewinski, this is Cheryl Brown from Harvey High School. I have two students in my office who would like to apply for the scholarship. Can you please mail the applications to me at the school at this address . . .these students are ready to apply and will meet the deadline. Thank you."

What's important about this scenario? How do you think Mr. Lewinsky responds to each person?

This scholarship administrator doesn't seem to embrace technology—no e-mail or voice mail. He prefers old-fashioned paper applications. He is probably a volunteer or very part-time worker at an organization that has priorities beyond the scholarship fund. How would you operate in order to meet the needs of this potential sponsor? Here are a few suggestions:

■ Asking this type of person to make exceptions for you is not a good way to start the process.

■ Mail means mail. E-mail means e-mail. Follow the directions.

■ A mistake on your part should not inconvenience the judges, but make every effort to correct the mistake, if possible. Some judges will accept missing materials late, others will not.

Office #2, Financial Aid Office at a Liberal Arts College

Josie Williams throws her workout bag in the corner of her office and sits down to check e-mail. Her inbox contains twenty messages and half of them are scholarship requests. She quickly attaches the application packet to outgoing e-mails and reminds people that the deadline is in one week—no exceptions. A member of the scholarship committee peeks in her office.

"Hi Josie. I'm going on vacation early next week. Can you make sure I get all of my copies of the applications by end of day Friday? Any good ones I should flag?" asks the committee member.

"A few students stand out but I'll let you take a look yourself. I'll also include the judging sheet so you can record your scores for each applicant. We've got thirty applicants already and I'm expecting a few more to come in by the deadline." Josie says. "I just have to verify their financial status."

"Remember last year?" says the committee member, "We had those two students who kept begging you and sending letters to every member of the committee? I'm so glad we found that other student. His essay rocked."

"I know. The good news is that this year's pool is solid so far. Good essays, good recommendations, and they all match the criteria. I think the judge's review lunch might even be fun. Hey, do you want to sign up for this other scholarship committee in the English department? They need more staff to review the applicants . . ."

What do you notice about this scenario? Who makes the decision about who wins? Is this person comfortable with technology? How is she different than the first example? Here are some suggestions for this scenario:

- Make sure you match the criteria and stand out.

- Decisions are made with a judging sheet by a committee. You might want to ask ahead of time how applicants will be scored, because different categories could have different weight in the total score.

- Be careful about the deadline. This person has already alerted students that there are no exceptions.

Office #3, Major National Scholarship Provider

As Tracy looks up from her desk, the mail clerk brings in another box of applicants. She flips through and sees postmarks from all over the country. At least a thousand students have applied online, but these students still prefer to mail it in. Next year students will be required to use the website for their applications because the scholarship board voted to eliminate paper applications. Tracy's assistant walks in.

"Good morning. Have you had a chance to plow through your e-mail yet? The podcast has been rescheduled and we need your approval," the assistant says.

"I'll check it and respond. How is the new computerized assessment tool working this week? Is it filtering the applicants and generating the thank-you letters on time?" Tracy asks.

"Yes. It's working great. You and the judges should have a list of the top 10 percent of applicants on Friday so we can review their essays. Sure beats reviewing them all one by one."

"I know. I'm using the extra time this year to prepare for the scholarship luncheon and media blitz. This is our biggest year ever—almost a quarter of a million dollars in scholarships."

What level of competition do you think you'd experience with this scholarship? How can you improve your odds? Here are some suggestions for this scenario:

■ It is important that you submit impeccable materials, free of typos or erroneous information, because a computer program is essentially monitoring and selecting finalists.

■ Your competition is more than one thousand students, so make sure you are highly qualified before you apply.

■ In this highly competitive scenario, the judges will read essays. Perfect your essay before you send it.

■ With online applications, be sure to proofread carefully before hitting the "send" button.

Your Plan

You need a personalized plan in order to excel at winning scholarships. Many students mistakenly underestimate their ability to influence scholarship judges. You have the ability to be successful if you are prepared—academically and administratively—and you invest in the process. How do you do that?

Before you apply for any scholarships, go back to your dream. Is it articulated well? Do you have key phrases that you can use in applications and essays? Your dream is the basis for everything else, so make sure it is a good one.

Is there anything else you can do to make yourself the best candidate possible for winning scholarships? Have you taken college-prep classes such as upper-level math, science, and English? Are you able to write a compelling, coherent essay? Scholarship applications rarely ask you to solve a math problem, but the majority will ask for an essay or require some compositional writing. If you are weak at writing, sharpen your skills through tutoring or take classes that will polish your essay-writing skills. This is an essential, nonnegotiable skill that can greatly influence your success.

ESSAYS MATTER!

Barbara and Don Goldberg's family established a scholarship fund to honor their dear friend, Barbara McCray, who passed away. Their friend was an African-American and Native American woman who grew up in Mississippi and never had the opportunity to go to college. She loved children and she loved gardening. Barbara and her family awarded the first scholarship to a young woman who met the criteria but did not have the highest academic rank among the applicants. Why? According to Ms. Goldberg, "Some students don't give the essay the care that it was meant to receive. The winner of our scholarship wasn't the strongest student but her essay meshed with who Barbara McCray was. We loved her essay."

In addition to the family scholarship, Ms. Goldberg serves on a panelist of judges who review applications for a statewide scholarship. With hundreds of potential applicants each year, the panel uses a point system as part of an objective process, but according to Ms. Goldberg, "The essays count a lot."

According to Ms. Goldberg, essays can make or break your application. Be sure that your essay is coherent and compelling if you want to increase your chance of winning scholarships. Objectivity is the rule for scholarship committees, but the reality is that judges are human beings who are subconsciously influenced by their own experiences and emotions—and by well-written essays that tell good stories.

My advice is that if your grade point averages in English and composition classes are less than 3.0, then plan to polish your skills. This is the single biggest investment you can personally make to prepare yourself for scholarship applications.

Your World Headquarters

Carve out space for your "office" or headquarters while applying for scholarships or you may quickly find yourself disorganized and buried in paperwork. Your headquarters could be a box under your bed, a corner of your desk, or one folder in your backpack. You might also put a folder in your kitchen or wherever your family opens the mail. For students who think they can apply for all scholarships online and keep electronic records of everything, you are ambitious but not realistic. The reality is that many scholarship providers still require paperwork, and most schools operate with a stream of paperwork, too. Students who "can't find it," whatever "it" is, are not going to have huge success winning scholarships. You must be organized if you plan on applying for and winning multiple scholarships. You want to be in control of your success. Don't think of it as paperwork; think of it as running your own small business. If you are entrepreneurial in the least, you will do well at this process.

What kind of office supplies will you need? If you have the essentials for school, you are probably ready for the scholarship-application process. Please invest in at least one folder that is devoted to scholarship materials. You will also need stamps, a small stapler, envelopes, thank-you notes or cards, and white computer paper. Your school's guidance department may have these items for you, with the exception of stamps and thank-you cards. If you need to purchase all of these items yourself, you can do so for less than ten dollars.

If you have a computer at home, that's great. Make a subfolder called "scholarships," or "cash for college," or whatever you deem an appropriate title. If you do not have your own computer, it is essential that you have a place to store your electronic information. Your school might allow this, or you can purchase a portable storage drive, often called a "jump" drive or "flash" drive, or some new technology that wasn't invented when I wrote this book. At the most basic level, a computer disk will work, too. You want something that is portable so you can work at home, school, or a library, if needed. You decide what format, but make sure that the storage mode you choose is permitted on the computers you will use.

Your Team and Its Role

Your next step is to determine who is on your team. If you try to do everything by yourself, perhaps out of necessity, prepare yourself for some serious work. I advocate that you find people (remember your Team of Champions?) to assist you. People can fulfill their roles if those roles are clearly outlined and people understand the larger purpose. Although many folks on your Team of Champions will serve as information gatherers and cheerleaders for your cause, you now need specific tasks accomplished.

Writing

You are the only person who can write the application and the essay. To assign this to someone else would be dishonest and put your whole effort in jeopardy. Students have actually asked me if someone else can fill out the applications for them. No. Period. If you want the money, then you fill out the application. Do not hire someone to do this. Do not download someone else's essay and tweak it for your purposes—it is unethical and it will catch up with you. I understand that families are desperate to pay for college, but nothing will sink your chance of getting into college or winning scholarship money faster than a hot essay.

Proofreading

A trusted friend, teacher, parent, or mentor can review the application for errors, misspellings, and clarity. Who will do this? Do you know someone? If not, it will be you. I suggest finding a few people for proofreading so that the joy (burden) of doing this doesn't rest on one person. What if your proofreader goes on vacation or can't respond in time? Think about this carefully and select two people. Lucky for me, my husband is a professional writer. My mother, however, is one of the worst spellers I know. Who am I going to trust to review my materials? I love my mom, but she knows my answer. If you plan to proofread all of your materials yourself, which I know is common, take a long break between revisions so you have fresh eyes.

Searching for Scholarships

Students who jump ahead to this step and spend most of their time surfing the Web for scholarships are making a mistake. They are aimless and don't really know what they are looking for. When they find a scholarship with a deadline quickly approaching, they aren't prepared. You will be prepared. That's what this chapter is all about. You will be the primary person searching for scholarships because you are the best person to do it. You know your strengths, weaknesses, and interests. You can multiply your prospect list, however, if you ask other people to scope out resources for you. Not just anybody—but people who have a personal interest in seeing you go to college.

My advice is to recruit the people who care most about you. Grandmas are some of my favorite people for this task. Why? Because they read the newspaper, visit with neighbors, and seem to know what's going on in the community. My grandma still tells me news about neighbors I had twenty-five years ago. How is that related to scholarships? She is a seeker and distributor of information. I know if I asked my grandma to watch the paper for anything related to scholarships, she would do it because she likes me and she likes to be helpful.

Another person who might be a viable assistant is a parent who knows almost everything about you. In my experience, moms and dads are some of the best scholarship seekers because they know the cost of college and they are petrified of paying that bill! Do a dance if your parents are on board and helping you. If you are a parent reading this book, give yourself a pat on the back.

If the parent-teenager relationship in your house is lukewarm, then I understand that parents might not be the best choice. I also understand that most parents work and they are busy people. If they are not the best choice, keep looking. Be careful, however, when you approach others, and think about what you say. "My parents aren't able to help me right now," is far better than, "My parents won't give me any help." Both statements might be true, but do you see the difference in tone? Remember to be positive when seeking help.

Your guidance counselor should know about the seriousness with which you are pursuing scholarships. Bring evidence of your efforts. Show your counselor this book and your notes and your dream. Your counselor may have hundreds of other students to assist, but it's worth asking for help. If your school doesn't have guidance counselors or college-transition coordinators, find a teacher or revisit your Team of Champions list. A letter or phone call from parents is a nice touch but, remember, counselors have hundreds of students. This should be a friendly call, not the "Get my kid some money or I'll have you fired" kind of call. Seriously.

Records

Students are the primary people to request records. Some records requests may need a parent's or guardian's signature. Don't be surprised by this and don't wait until the last minute. You will also need to rely on the staff at your school, most likely the guidance secretary or main office secretary. Be nice to these people, because it's the right thing to do and because they can make or break your attempt to get records in a timely fashion. In the business world, these folks are called "gatekeepers," and they are known for their power to move things along or slow them down. Give them every reason to like you and assist you without bribing them, of course.

Photocopying

Your school guidance office or library may allow students free or low-cost photocopying of scholarship-application materials. Parents might be able to make a few copies at work, if the boss doesn't mind, but it can be a pain taking things back and forth. Look for a nearby public library, post office, gas station, or copying business that has good machines that make clear copies. Make a copy of all final applications before you submit them to the sponsors, because applications really do get lost in the mail—or in someone's office— and you should have your own copy as a backup. Someone needs to be in charge of photocopies. Who will it be?

Mailing

Online submissions require a thorough review of your application, but after that you hit the submit button and violà—your application is delivered in seconds. For sponsors who are still fond of paper applications (that is, most of them), students are required to mail the materials. Check the fine print to see if the deadline is a *postmark date*, which is the date stamped by the Post Office, or a *received-by* date, which is the date materials must arrive at the sponsor's address. Did you remember to buy stamps? Are you going to wait in line twenty minutes at the post office every time you need another three stamps? Before you put one measly stamp on a fat envelope containing twelve pages of paper, all required for the scholarship, take the time to weigh the envelope and make sure you have enough postage. Don't let fifty cents stand between you and your potential scholarship money. Be prepared with the postage.

Who will be responsible for mailing the applications? You may laugh at the simplicity of this step but students, parents, counselors, and friends can easily get confused about who will mail the applications. I always prefer to mail my documents myself. I like to watch them drop in the mail chute and then I have no one else to blame about a late postmark. Your school may have an arrangement with a sponsor whereby the school can mail all the applications at once. If so, take advantage of this time- and money-saving luxury.

Scheduling

A big step in your plan to win scholarships is understanding when applications are due, how long it takes to write an essay, and how much time you need to give the folks who are helping you. This can be complex or simple depending on the number of scholarships on your list.

February, March, and April are the busiest months for completing scholarship applications. Other forms of financial aid have springtime deadlines, and many colleges use March 1 as a preferred deadline for completion of the FAFSA. *If you wait until June of your senior year to apply for scholarships, you will have missed the majority of opportunities for fall-semester funding.* No matter when you are reading this book, my advice is simple: start now.

Why are applications due six months prior to your college enrollment date? Sponsors need time to judge materials, conduct interviews if necessary, announce the winners, and allocate the funds, all in time for you to go to college. They might even squeeze in a banquet or luncheon to showcase the winners.

Your strategy for success is to develop a calendar system that clearly shows your deadlines and the minideadlines that will allow you to submit a full application. Work backward from each deadline to assemble the materials you need.

Develop a Time Predictor

No, this isn't a creation from science fiction, it's a tool to help you schedule time for your scholarship applications. At the most basic level, I figure that the number of pages on the application is about the number of hours it will take you to complete it, plus additional time to write the essay and secure letters of recommendation.

101

Sure, that one page looks like it will take ten minutes, but it requires you to gather information, get signatures, check for typos, make copies, etc. It all adds up. For your first letter of recommendation, allot one hour. For your first essay, plan on several hours, spread over multiple days or weeks. After you build the body of your best essay, you can use it multiples times with revisions for each specific provider. Allot one additional hour each time your revise it for a specific scholarship sponsor. Here's an example:

- One page application = one hour. (Gather information, fill in the blanks, get signatures, and make copies.)

- One letter of recommendation = one hour. (Discuss with the teacher, provide information, answer questions, and collect the letter. Your role may take one hour, but it could take the recommender days or weeks to get the letter back to you.)

- First essay = three to five hours. (Varies greatly depending on the length of the essay and your writing skills. It could take twice as long.)

That's seven hours for your first one-page application. This assumes you have your personal information readily available to complete the application, and you will add time to stop at the post office. The next application process will probably go faster.

Students who complete one application and think, "That took way too long," don't realize that the first application usually takes the longest because it's all new to you! As you become a scholarship guru, orchestrating the perfect system of people and paperwork, you will cut your time significantly.

P.S.: These are very rough estimates. Create your own time predictor based on your work style and the pace at which you write.

— — — — — — — — — — — — — — — — — — — —

Final Plan

Your dreams will only get you so far. Grunt work is required. That's the real world. Students who are successful at securing cash for college have a plan. One student I met, Minh, devoted nearly every Saturday of her senior year to preparing herself, searching for scholarships, asking for help, working on her essay, and applying for scholarships. Most students skip the preparation and fall into the myth that anyone can get a scholarship by filling out lots of applications. The most successful students take it seriously, treat it like a business, and have a plan. Minh was able to raise more than $30,000 from her efforts.

— — — — — — — — — — — — — — — — — —

Quick Terms

Financial Need: A general term used to capture the many factors that determine family income level and the student's ability to pay for college. The government will provide an estimated family contribution (EFC) after the applicant submits a FAFSA, but scholarship providers may use their own methods of determining need.

Letter of Recommendation: A letter written by someone who admires you and can testify to your scholarship worthiness.

Nomination Form: A document completed by someone who has the power and authority to recommend you for a scholarship. This may or may not accompany letters of recommendation.

Transcript: A school's or school district's official record of a student's courses and grades.

— — — — — — — — — — — — — — — — — —

MORE THAN $30,000 TO ATTEND A BIG TEN SCHOOL!

Minh moved to America from Vietnam when she was three years old. Her parents both had college degrees, but they worked at factory jobs in America because of language barriers.

In Minh's family, college was not a choice—it was a requirement. She knew from a young age that her parents expected her to earn a degree. She was most inspired by her mother, who had been a pharmacist in Vietnam.

Minh earned more than $30,000 in scholarships to attend the University of Wisconsin-Madison, a Big Ten school. She attributes her success to participating in Upward Bound, a precollege program where the staff helped to motivate her and support her with her plans to go to college. They convinced Minh to join student government and school activities, and to try volunteer work. Her parents couldn't help her with homework or offer advice about applying to college, but Upward Bound did.

Minh and Allan, two successful scholarship winners.

She received free tutoring and advice about personal issues during her senior year.

With fierce determination, Minh devoted nearly every Saturday for six months to preparing her résumé, applications, and essays for scholarships. She began her search at a national level by using well-known websites, and she applied for the Gates Millennium Scholarship. She didn't win. But the Upward Bound staff would not let her give up.

She then focused on local scholarships and found the UW-Madison Chancellor's Scholarship, which offered four years of full tuition. She didn't receive the application packet until three days before the deadline, and the day it was supposed to be postmarked her parents' car broke down. She called her aunt and uncle, who drove her to the post office in time to get the official postmark required for the scholarship application. Two months later she was notified that she won the scholarship. She was so grateful and excited that Minh said she "cried and cried" when she heard the news.

Minh also earned three other local scholarships. Minh's advice to other students is, "Pour your soul into your essay," and, "If you are running out of time, go for local scholarships—your chances are much better."

Minh acknowledges that many people helped her achieve success, including family members, school staff, and her precollege advisors. "Most people want to help you," Minh said. "If you stumble on someone who won't, then find someone else, but you have to give them respect, too."

Fridge Notes

Class Notes: Forming Your Plan

1. Is your dream ready to go?

2. Have you invested in yourself? What else do you need to do? Test prep? Work on writing skills?

3. Set up your world headquarters and gather your supplies.

   a. Folder or binder

   b. Stamps

   c. Stapler

   d. Envelopes

   e. Thank-you notes

   f. White computer paper

   g. Electronic storage

4. Make sure your Team of Champions is ready to go.

5. Divide the work. Will it be just you or anyone else? (Fill in the blanks.)

   a. Writing: <u>You</u>

   b. Proofreading _____

   c. Searching for scholarships_____

   d. Requesting and keeping records_____

   e. Photocopies _____

   f. Postage and mailing_____

   g. Scheduling_____

6. Are you ready?

Load Up Your Backpack

My goal in this chapter is to help you create personalized tools and tactics that are effective and save you time. You will also focus on searching for scholarships. Each scholarship provider may ask for different versions of the same information. It is in your best interest to have everything ready to go so you can streamline the process and increase your number of high-quality applications. Treat every scholarship application like a mini open-book exam. You need your notes, your book, your homework, etc. to do the best job. It's all the same content, just different formats. To prepare, imagine filling your backpack with everything you need before you take the exam.

In one part of my career I was responsible for raising money to operate the education programs that I managed. During that time, I learned how to use standardized copy and statistics and transform them to meet the needs of potential donors. Likewise, to find an agent and publisher for this book, I had to pitch the same idea to different audiences. For each new person, I modified my proposal or added information specifically about him or her. Agents and publishers are much like the scholarship sponsors that you will encounter—they read hundreds or perhaps thousands of proposals (applications), and they only pick a few. Why not yours?

Scholarship Worksheet Brainstorming

The first tool you will create is your personalized scholarship worksheet. It will serve two purposes. First, it will help you identify all aspects of your personal and academic life that may lead to a scholarship. Second, it will provide a snapshot of your success to your helpers and to decision makers. Therefore, you're going to invest significantly in crafting your scholarship worksheet.

"Is this going to be a lot of work?" you ask. Yes, but it's worth it. You will use the scholarship worksheet during the scholarship exploration process. It may be anywhere from one to four pages long, depending on your level of activity and unique characteristics of you and your family. You definitely want to share this with your Team of Champions or family members. If someone says, "This is way too long," your reply should be, "I will have a traditional résumé too, but on this scholarship worksheet I wanted to include everything that could possibly match me with a scholarship."

How do you create a scholarship worksheet? You begin by gathering information about yourself in two realms: your academic life and your personal life. On a piece of paper, create two columns: one titled "academics" and the other titled "personal." This piece of paper is your rough draft for the scholarship worksheet. At this stage, you are brainstorming and gathering information, so don't worry about forming proper sentences. Simply list your achievements.

To begin, think about your life. How can you categorize who you are and how you spend your time? How can you set yourself apart from the competition?

Your Academic Life

You need a clear picture of your academic performance. You will repeat this information across the applications, and it is not okay to guess. "I *think* I have a 3.2 GPA," isn't going to cut it, because the students you're competing with will know their exact grade point averages.

Many applications require a high school transcript, and you need to check that the GPA you report on the application matches the GPA on your transcript. What are your scores on the ACT or SAT tests? Have you received special academic recognition? Are you a member of the National Honor Society, National Art Honor Society, or another academic group? Think about your involvement. Were you a member, organizer, or leader? What was your role? If you took Advanced Placement or honors classes, list them in the "academics" column along with your final grades. Have you completed academic enrichment classes or tutoring? Anything related to school or college preparation should be documented in the "academics" column. At this stage, focus on making the list. Later, you will use the list to design a scholarship worksheet, to find scholarships, and to build your essay.

Is your list long or short? Are you forgetting anything? If you have been keeping a profile or folder of your accomplishments throughout high school, then this task can be accomplished in about thirty minutes. If you have never gathered and documented this information, it can take a few hours or a few days, depending on your level of involvement at school and the ease of retrieving the information. The most important things are to be thorough and to be accurate.

Your Personal Life

On the same piece of paper, under the "personal" column heading, list everything about you and your family that defines who you are. List your race, ethnicity, gender, where you were born, and the city or town where you live now; your high school, clubs, sports, and activities (outside of school, too); your jobs, places of employment, and volunteer work; and your parents' places of employment, alma maters (if they graduated), volunteer work, or their memberships in rotary clubs, unions, neighborhood associations, and veterans organizations. Your parents' involvement in the community can lead to scholarship opportunities for you. For example, the American Legion and the American Legion Auxiliary offer dozens of scholarships, but if no one in your family is involved in these organizations, how would you know about their scholarships? Here's another example of documenting your family's characteristics: If your dad leads the neighborhood crime-watch group and you help him send out e-mails, organize the meetings, and make the newsletter—that's volunteer work! Write down the name of the crime-watch group and include any official affiliations it may have with the city government, such as the "Department of City Development." Maybe you haven't thought about it like that before.

"Hey Scholarship Lady, my mom and dad don't do anything like that. Now what?" you might be thinking. Dig deeper is my advice. Every human being has a story to tell. If your dad has been farming the same land that's been in your family for a hundred years, write that down. Does your mom work part-time at a retail store? Sometimes major retailers offer scholarships to the children of employees; in other cases, they prohibit employees' families from applying for the scholarships. These are the details that other people might not know about you and your family. These details could lead to scholarships or at the very least, might inspire part of your essays. A student's like or dislike of his or her parent's career choices can be very motivating. You may want to follow in your parents' footsteps or completely avoid their lines of work.

If your parents were members of an organization but quit because they were too busy, maybe they would consider reactivating their membership for networking purposes. Ask your parents if they have any memberships in community organizations or clubs.

- -

HOT TIP

Attention parents: Do you belong, or did you ever belong, to a civic or cultural group such as an Irish dance troupe, Italian community center, amateur radio club, Swedish-American club, Daughters of the American Revolution, Lions Club, Hmong Women's Professional Circle, Moose Lodge, Jewish community center, Hispanic Chamber of Commerce, African-American fraternities/sororities, or other clubs? Even if you haven't been involved in years, scholarships abound at these types of organizations and you might want to touch base with your old buddies or reactivate your memberships. How will you know about their scholarship dollars if you are not there?

101

- -

Still nothing about the parents? That's okay. Your academic and personal profiles are the most important. Your parents' connections are just icing on the cake. A cake with no icing is still cake, right?

Now you should have two lists on your piece of paper: one based on your academic profile and one based on your personal profile. The next step is to assemble them into your scholarship worksheet.

Scholarship Worksheet Format

After brainstorming, you move into assembly mode. The scholarship worksheet should be typed on a computer and should use the results of the academic and personal lists you just finished. A basic format is fine. Put your name and contact information at the top. Create headings to mark the different sections of your worksheet. If you don't have any information to put under these suggested headings, just skip that section. Review the snapshot of the sample scholarship worksheet in figure 6–1. Realize that some sections may have only one sentence and others might have multiple paragraphs. You might skip sections if you have no information. That's understandable. No one expects you to list an entire page of job experience. You may, however, list an entire page of activities if you've been busy.

Create an "Academics" Heading

List your high school and expected year of graduation followed by your achievements such as your grade point average and test scores.

Create an "Awards and Honors" Heading

If you've received awards or special distinctions, document them with the year and the honor. If not, skip it. No big deal.

Create an "Employment" or "Experience" Heading

List any jobs you've had, including your employer name, title, basic responsibilities, and the employment dates. If your boss liked you and you did a good job, list the boss's name and phone number for reference. Babysitting is a job, even if you are watching your little sister, and you should include it on the worksheet. Many students can't work after-school jobs, because they have responsibilities at home, and scholarship judges know that. This might also help explain to your counselors and teachers why you don't hang around after school. Remember, this worksheet is to let people know a little bit more about you. If you don't have a job, you might want to

Morgan M. Robinson
98766 Hope Blvd.
Big Creek, NM 20034
(555) 342–8456
morganmr@yourmail.com

Academics

Big Creek High School   *September 2005–present*
Expected graduation: 2009
GPA: 3.19
ACT SCORE: 29

Enrolled in college-prep curriculum since freshman year.

Employment

Alfredo's Pizza   *June 2008–present*
Part-time Cashier. Responsible for taking orders, accepting payments, and balancing the drawer at the end of my shift. Twice awarded Employee of the Month by the manager.
Supervisor: Mac Billings
Phone: 342–1276

Community Service

Fourth Street Food Pantry   *December 2006–present*
Food Sorter. Once a month sort food and rotate stock. Conduct inventory and assemble care packages.
Supervisor varies.

Memberships

Multicultural Club   *September 2005–June 2007*
Secretary. Organized monthly meetings and wrote monthly summaries. Founder of the annual multicultural holiday showcase. Voted to represent our school at the statewide multicultural student conference.

Activities and Interests

Big Creek Cheerleaders   *September 2005–December 2008*
Football Cheerleader   Fall 2005, 2006, 2007
Team Captain   Fall 2008
Cheered at every football game during the past four years. Started as a freshman, moved up to JV and then varsity. Voted team captain. Captain duties included organizing a fund-raiser that resulted in $500 for our school. Provided leadership such as uniform selection, scheduling practices and workouts, managing a food drive, and securing sponsors for the homecoming parade. Led our team to win the state cheerleading championship—a first in school history.

[Continued . . .]

Figure 6–1. Partial sample of scholarship worksheet.

list other experience such as an internship or study-abroad experience. If you don't have a job or any other unique experiences, skip it.

Create a "Volunteer Work" or "Community Service" Heading

Use the same format as the employment section: place/organization, title, duties, and dates. Again, list your supervisor and the phone number, if relevant. If your supervisors have e-mail addresses, list those too. If you only volunteered somewhere once, along with hundreds of other people, perhaps at a rally or walk, it's not important to go into great detail.

HOT TIP

Eligibility vs. Award Criteria

". . . Must have a 3.0 GPA, exhibit leadership skills, and plan to attend a four-year college. Proof of community service is important," you read from the application. "Great, that's me!" you think. I could win this scholarship. What you have just read is eligibility criteria, but it's not the award criteria. People who meet those minimum requirements are invited to apply, but will they win?

101

For you to gain an edge in winning scholarships, you want to know the *award* criteria. These are the guidelines scholarship judges use to discern who will win the scholarship. The guidelines may or may not appear on the application. If they do, you will see a description about what is important to the judges. It could be percentages or points that will be awarded for each section of your application. If it's not clear to you what the award criteria is, visit the sponsor's website or call and ask. One question might be, "Hi, I'm interested in applying for your scholarship and want to do my best job. I'd like to know if certain parts of the application have more weight than others during the judging process." Pay attention to the answer and use that knowledge to craft a better application.

Create a "Memberships" Heading

If you are a member of, or have been a representative of, a club or association, put it on the list. List all official memberships as opposed to your activities. For example, if you write for the school newspaper, that is an *activity* to be listed in the next section. If your school has a journalism *club*, however, and you are a *member*, list it in the "Memberships" section. This will provide more evidence of your commitment to journalism, and sometimes national organizations have college and high school affiliates. In order to apply for their scholarships, you must be a member.

Worksheet Wording

Let's imagine that you started your own business providing computer tech support over the summer. That would be a job. You should put it in the "Employment" section. If you build websites for fun, that's a hobby and you should list it in the "Activities" section. If you are a member of the Media and Technology Club at your school, that goes under "Memberships." Perhaps your combination of entrepreneurship and love of computers led you to join Future Business Leaders of America (FBLA). If you are a member of FBLA, that would also go under "Memberships."

Why am I spending so much time dividing up your love of computers? Because it is essential to look at every possible angle for scholarships. Your love of computers is not unique; however, if you joined the Media and Technology Club at school and you opened your own business, you have sound evidence that you are a little more serious about hard drives, software, programming, or mechanics than your fellow computer aficionados (I would never call you a computer geek). If you took the additional step to join FBLA, you just joined an organization that offers awards and scholarships to high school students with strong business skills and an entrepreneurial spirit. See the connections: you + computers + work + activities + membership = scholarship.

Create an "Activities and Interests" Heading

Name the activity and list your title, duties (or what you did), and the dates you were involved. If you are on a waterskiing team, that's an out-of-school activity worthy of documentation. If you collect antique dolls, that's an interest that you should also document. For formal activities, you need to give people an accurate account of your achievements. Sometimes simple phrases are the best, and sometimes you need to explain with details. How you craft your language now will affect how people view your accomplishments.

You've Got Spirit, Yes You Do!

Let's take cheerleading for an example of how to document your activities. Are you just a cheerleader or a supercheerleader? Here are a few examples of how to list this on your scholarship worksheet:

Good: Varsity Football Cheerleader. Cheer at all football games, 2004–2008.

Better: Football Cheerleader. Freshman, JV, and varsity member, 2004–2008. Cheer at all football games. Voted team captain in 2008.

Better Than That: Football Cheerleader, 2004–2007. Team Captain, 2008. Cheered at every football game during the past four years. Started as a freshman, moved up to JV and then varsity. Voted team captain. Captain duties included organizing a fund-raiser that resulted in $500 for our school. Provided leadership such as uniform selection, scheduling practices and workouts, managing a food drive, and securing sponsors for the homecoming parade. Led our team to win the state cheerleading championship—a first in school history.

Be careful as you do this because you don't want to sound phony. Skip the fluff and go for the facts. Notice I didn't say, "Save the world one cheer at a time." It makes me cringe just to type that. My "Better Than That" example shows people who aren't familiar with cheerleading some of the extras that come with being a team captain. It shows that the captain is responsible, reliable, and a team player. Using the word *voted* shows that your peers believed in you. Also notice I didn't call the last version my "Best" example. That's because résumé writing is subjective and you might come up with an "Even Better Than That" version.

Create a "Personal Traits" Heading

List the things about you that other people might not know. Think about any disabilities or other conditions affecting you and your family. These conditions or situations could be positive or negative, but the point is to list the things that other students may not have experienced. Your unique traits will help you unearth the harder-to-find scholarships that are reserved for people like you. If you are an academically talented tall person and you apply for the Tall Club scholarship, then being tall no longer sets you apart. Your other traits will be given greater consideration.

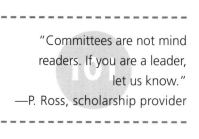

"Committees are not mind readers. If you are a leader, let us know."

—P. Ross, scholarship provider

Brainstorm About Your Traits

Think about who you are as you complete your scholarship worksheet. See if you can identify with any of these categories: foster child, adopted child, hearing-impaired, dyslexic, child of a cancer survivor, cancer patient, child of a disabled veteran, immigrant, survivor of a catastrophe, tall person, short person, a little person, left-handed, parents unemployed, homeless, single parent, child of a single parent, youngest/first/only person in your family to (fill in the blank). Be creative and list every possible trait about you.

In another example, if you are an immigrant, realize this is a hot-button issue in the news. Your immigration status, country of origin, when you immigrated, and your parents' status could all affect how you are perceived. Many organizations support immigrants as they build their new lives in America—other organizations oppose this support. Both might offer scholarships. For example, my father was an immigrant from Lithuania in the 1940s; he was orphaned at the age of twelve. A Lithuanian Club might find this interesting; others probably won't care. In this example and in others, realize that your unique factors could help, hinder, or have no effect on your scholarship success. It depends on the beliefs of the sponsoring organization.

Don't Be *Too* Unique

Let's concentrate on the word *unique*. Besides being the most overused word in the scholarship business (I admit it!), it can have unintended effects. Throughout the scholarship process you will be advised to emphasize how you are unique compared with other applicants, but when is being unique the demise of your application?

Some scholarship judges don't want to give money to anyone who strays too far from their own beliefs or from the beliefs of the organizations they represent. After all, it's their money. If you are applying for a scholarship in the health care industry and you wrote an essay about the positive effects of alternative medicine, will the judges be receptive to that? It depends. If someone in your family has experienced relief from a medical condition by using alternative medicine, and the scholarship sponsor is an association of alternative medicine practitioners, you could be successful. How would sponsors from a traditional hospital or a pharmaceutical company view your essay? Again, it depends. If the chair of the scholarship committee just appeared on the nightly news arguing against alternative therapies, praise for your essay is unlikely.

Think about what you want to say, but think about your audience, too. Just because you are passionate about a cause does not mean that every audience wants to hear about it. Think carefully about your unique traits before you use them in your scholarship plan.

Beware of Bragging vs. Informing

Providing ample evidence of your scholarship worthiness without bragging too much is a difficult skill. Few adults have mastered this—yet I am asking you to do it! I know this is a colossal task, but it will open up so many more opportunities if you document your achievements and think creatively about how you spend your time. Let me give you one more example.

I once received a phone call from a college student who was seeking advice. She had applied for fifteen scholarships but did not win a single penny. I learned that she had "above average" grades but was a very average person. She grew up in a small town, went to college in a big city, attended a nursing program, worked on campus, and volunteered with the Red Cross. All pretty normal stuff. No wonder she was having a hard time. As she told me about her efforts, I asked her more about the Red Cross volunteer work. What does she do? Is it often? Once in a while? Her response was very simple: "I volunteer at the festivals."

These festivals that she mentioned attract nearly a million people a year who listen to bands, dance on picnic tables, people-watch, and more. Novice festivalgoers can be ill-prepared for the heat or become victims of a stage dive. People may suffer sunstroke, dehydration, concussions, bloody noses, sprained ankles, or a variety of other ailments. Her volunteer job was on the mobile-response team that assisted those ailing festivalgoers. It was a serious job with a high level of responsibility, but the language she had been using to describe it was simply "Red Cross volunteer."

Think about the scholarship judges. They don't know you and they can't possibly know the nuances of every activity in which you participate. The nursing student I described was far from bragging. I had to question her and pull out the fabulous facts of her volunteer work. I wondered what else I didn't know. You need to balance bragging about yourself and showcasing your unique and wonderful traits with a small dose of humility. If you don't brag somewhat, then judges won't know how great you are. If you don't throw in a spoonful of humility, then you are just a braggart. Students who balance the two are the gems of the scholarship world, and judges love them.

Create the "Parents" or "Family Information" Heading

This is your last section. Look at your two-column brainstorming list, take information about your parents from the "personal" column, and put it in this section. In addition to your parents' places of employment, list their military service, if any. Assure your parents that you aren't trying to be disrespectful or intrusive when you quiz them about their pasts; you are simply trying to find any possible connection to a scholarship. Ask your grandparents, too. Employers, unions, universities, and civic groups may offer scholarships for the grandchildren of their staff, members, or alumni.

A sample parent entry might look like this:

Mother: Cindy Robinson

Work: U.S. Postal Service, 2002–present

Education: Gateway Technical College, associate's degree in data management, 1983

Memberships:

Gardenvale Booster Club, 1999–present

St. Paul's Catholic Church, 1980–present

American Postal Workers Union, 2002–present

AMF Bowling League, 2005–2007

Take a look. Do you see any potential scholarship opportunities? I do. Colleges sometimes offer scholarships to the children of alumni (people who graduated from the college). Civic clubs, churches, and unions are good places to find scholarships, too. Last, if you have any inclination to go bowling, do it! If you are any good at it, you might consider joining a league and becoming a member of a bowling organization. Why? It is one more way to set yourself apart from the competition, and (drumroll please) according to the United States Bowling Congress more than $2.7 million is available in tournament awards and scholarships. *Caution: If you choose to pursue bowling scholarships, you must observe athletic regulations so as not to jeopardize your ability to play sports at your high school.* Ask a coach at your school. If you love bowling, it's worth it to pursue your interest.

HOT TIP

You Don't Know If You Don't Ask

Remember when I told you that I applied for one scholarship from a women's club and didn't win? Don't worry, the pity party didn't last forever. I was able to secure tuition assistance from two of my employers. Basically, it was free money for college and I didn't have to fill out an application or write an essay.

101

How did I do it? I scheduled a meeting with my supervisors, built my strongest case for why they should help me pay for tuition (because they would benefit from my newfound knowledge, of course), and they paid. I felt comfortable doing this because I had always received praise and support from these supervisors in the past.

Few high school students could do this with an employer, but I share the story with you to illustrate three points: (1) I had nothing to lose, and everything to gain, by simply asking; (2) there was a benefit for them; and (3) you and your parents should check with employers about scholarships *and* tuition-assistance programs.

Scholarship Worksheet Review

To wrap up your scholarship worksheet, look closely at each section and determine if you included every possible connection to a scholarship. Are there any areas that you could improve or add to in the next few months? If you share this document with your Team of Champions, will it be easy to understand? What types of scholarships would be good matches?

Congratulations on finishing this task!

I'd like to revisit the concept of your Fabulous Factor. As you look over your accomplishments, think about your competition locally and nationally. I want you to think about how you measure up compared with students in your school, your city, your state, and across the country. This can be a very encouraging exercise or a very humbling one. What I want you to understand is that judges are making their decisions based on the

YOU and your competitive field	1 **Extremely fabulous.** You stand out from others. Scholarship judges put you at the **top of the list.**	2 **Simply fabulous.** Better than most. Might make it into consideration, **depending on the competition.**	3 **Somewhat fabulous.** You stand out, but not the "total package." Judges put you in the **maybe pile.**	4 **Not fabulous.** You met the criteria and applied but **other students were more impressive.**	Notes
Your school					
Your city					
Your state					
Your country					

Figure 6–2. Fabulous Factor worksheet.

pool of applicants, not just one. You won't share this with anyone, but just for kicks, put one checkmark in each row of figure 6–2 to indicate your Fabulous Factor.

Your Scholarship Résumé

Your scholarship résumé will be a general, condensed version of your scholarship worksheet. It is a more traditional overview of your academic accomplishments and awards, work experience, volunteer service, memberships, and activities. Some scholarship applications or award programs may ask you to attach a synopsis of your achievements. The scholarship résumé fulfills that requirement. It is a professional, organized glimpse of your accomplishments.

To start your scholarship résumé, follow the same format as the scholarship worksheet. You can copy and paste to save time. List your personal information at the top, including your name and contact information. Next, list your education or academic information, followed by awards or honors. List your work experience and community service, followed by memberships, activities, and interests. *Condense the information from your scholarship worksheet.* Add a new section titled "References," which is where you will list two or three nonfamily members who can attest to your ambition, achievements, reliability, or other positive characteristics about you.

Fit this information on one page. On résumés, brevity counts; therefore weigh the importance of every word. Construct active instead of passive sentences, and speak in terms of your accomplishments.

For your résumé, do not include very personal information that appeared on the worksheet. The worksheet is a dynamic tool for your *team*; the résumé presents your image to the *public*. It is irrelevant to most people whether you are tall or short, adopted or not. Do not include any information about your parents or grandparents on the résumé. This résumé is all business and the purpose is to provide the reader with the most glowing, yet accurate, picture of what you've accomplished.

This résumé should take less than one hour or about one class period to complete if you use your scholarship worksheet as your starting point. It's worth it. Next time you are in study hall, maybe you can use the computers. Be sure to set a deadline to create this résumé. When will you do this? Today? Next week? Before bed? Saturday morning? The beauty is that you are in charge and you get to decide. Pick a time, promise yourself, and *act* upon your promise.

Fridge Notes

Scholarships 101 Backpack Checklist

❏ Scholarship worksheet brainstorming

- Your academic life: who are you?

  _____

  _____

  _____

- Your personal life: who are *you*, your *parents*, your *family*?

  _____

  _____

  _____

  _____

  _____

  (This will require you to talk with your parents. Text messaging about family history can be difficult.)

❏ Scholarship worksheet formatting

- Use proactive versus passive language.
- Use details that showcase your Fabulous Factor.
- Inform, don't brag.

❏ Scholarship résumé

- Create a nice, neat, condensed version of your worksheet.
- Remember to remove very personal information about your family.

Chapter 7

The Search Is On

The Internet is the fastest, cheapest way to get the most scholarship information. It represents a dump truck of opportunity that will reward the steadfast and savvy student who can figure out how to pluck the shiny apple out from the garbage. What if you're not steadfast or savvy? How do you avoid all the rotten apples or the ones that don't match what you need?

You need a plan to divide and conquer the scholarship pile. Only part of that plan involves the Internet. The rest involves networking with the people around you, meeting with your guidance counselor, and doing research at the library. You should also familiarize yourself with scholarship terminology before you begin. Check out the sidebar for descriptions.

Eligibility and Award Categories

Scholarship sponsors devise eligibility and award criteria to meet their goals for scholarships. Once you understand these categories, you will begin to absorb scholarship information faster and target which ones are the best matches for you. As you begin to use databases, books, or lists of scholarships, think about these terms and how they relate to your accomplishments. Some scholarships may use these terms and others may have different terminology.

Alumni-Sponsored Scholarship: A scholarship offered by the graduates of a college or university who contributed money to sponsor the scholarship.

Community-Service Scholarship: Scholarships based on students' achievements in volunteer work, community organizing, service learning, or other activities that benefit your community.

Economically Disadvantaged: A status of student or family income. Usually refers to low-income families but could include families who are facing significant financial instability.

Ethnicity-Based Criteria: A factor in eligibility or award criteria that clearly states the ethnicity of the students for whom the scholarship was intended.

Faculty-Sponsored Scholarship: A scholarship funded by the faculty at a university or by faculty within a certain department.

Leadership Scholarships: Scholarships based on students' proven roles as leaders in their schools or communities.

Merit-Based or Achievement-Based: The primary criteria for a scholarship based on academic achievements, possibly measured by GPA, class rank, and test scores.

Minority Scholarships: Scholarships targeting traditionally defined minority groups such as, but not limited to, African-American, Asian-American, Hispanic, Latino, or Native American/American Indian.

Need-Based Aid: Financial aid sources offered to students based on their level of financial need.

Need-Blind: A method whereby funds are awarded without regard to a student's financial needs.

Preference: An inclination toward a certain type of student, but if those students don't apply or don't impress the judges, the scholarship committee may select another student.

Race-Blind: A method of awarding financial aid whereby race is *not* a factor in eligibility or award criteria.

Traditionally Underrepresented Group: Students who, historically, have not enrolled in a particular college or program. Note: Colleges and universities realize that minority groups, when combined, now form a majority. "Traditionally underrepresented groups" is one way to acknowledge that people in minority groups, who traditionally do not attend college at the same rate as Caucasians, are no longer a minority. Another example is women who enter fields traditionally chosen by men. As a scholarship seeker, think about it like this: If you are an African-American student and you attend Morehouse College, you are *not* a traditionally underrepresented student at that college, but you *would be* considered a traditionally underrepresented student at most colleges in America.

HOT TIP

The Scoop on Preferences

There are two ways that preferences are commonly used in scholarships. First they are used as a recruitment tool: the donors have a clear picture in their minds of whom they want to receive their money, and they promote the scholarship to that group of people. If a strong candidate from that pool doesn't emerge, they will consider giving the scholarship to another strong candidate who might not fit the preference but meets all of the other criteria. For example, a sponsor might say, "Preference given to students who are the first in their family to attend college," but what if those students didn't apply? The sponsor may choose to award the scholarship to

101

other applicants who closely match the profile of the students they were seeking.

Second, preferences are used as an award tool. If everything is equal among the top applicants, the sponsor will award the scholarship to the student who meets the preferred criteria. For instance, geographic preferences are common. A sponsor might say, "All eligible students should apply, but a preference will be given to students from Marin county." It means that qualified students from Marin county will get the first round of money, but if few students from Marin county impress the judges, they may award the money to qualified students from other counties.

The distinction is subtle but important for scholarship seekers. You are most likely to win a scholarship in these scenarios if (1) you meet the preferences and submit a strong application, (2) your competition doesn't apply, or (3) if competitors did apply but submitted weak applications.

You should apply for these scholarships if you match the preference. You should also apply if you closely match the preference and have extra time to do it. If the scholarship guidelines list certain required criteria that you don't meet, then don't apply. Save your time for better matches.

Getting Started

Remember our bull's eye from chapter 3? Your first step in finding scholarships is not, I repeat, is not, to fry your eyes until midnight searching the Internet. That will come later. The first step is to talk with the people in your immediate circle who know about scholarships. Start in your school's guidance office, and if you don't have a guidance office, ask a teacher or school secretary.

You should start at your school first because much of what you will find on the Internet probably already exists at your school. Want to know the most popular scholarships at your school? Ask before you search. Remember that counselors and secretaries are the recipients and gatekeepers of college-bound information. Your school may maintain its own scholarship Web page, booklet, or list to give you a jump start. Also ask about announcements or newsletters from previous years that may feature scholarship winners. This experience will help you see what resources your school already has available. Your school district or state might maintain a searchable database of local scholarships, although this is rare. Boston, Massachusetts, and Milwaukee, Wisconsin, host the most robust locally grown scholarship databases that I've used. (To be honest, I helped create the one in Milwaukee, Wisconsin). Because websites are always subject to change, I will put the URLs on my website (www.scholarshipstreet.com). If you are aware of a strong, local database of scholarships and want me to know about it, just submit the name at my website.

What should you do if your school lacks scholarship information? Part of the Small Schools Initiative across the country has left some schools ill-prepared to provide meaningful scholarship help because no one is assigned this job. If you are not finding the information or support that you need, don't give up. You have several other ways to get the information you need.

Your next step is to turn to your Team of Champions. Let folks know that your search has begun. Visit them, make a call, send an e-mail, or send a text message. If you don't tell them about your search for scholarships, how else will they know? Provide your scholarship worksheet to your Team of Champions and ask if they have any questions. Now the real search can begin.

Scammers, Creeps, and Thugs

Okay, enough name-calling. In the scholarship profession, the deceitful people who prey upon scholarship-seeking students and their families are called scholarship scam artists. I added the new labels "creeps and thugs" because that's what they really are. Their sole purpose is to prey upon confused students and parents. Period.

According to the Federal Trade Commission, in 2004, about one percent of fraud complaints were related to scholarship scam artists. That doesn't sound like a lot, unless you were one of the victims. Use your street smarts to avoid these folks who may operate online, in person, via e-mail, or via snail mail. Just like comic book villains, the scammers can shift form to elude the good guys, so stay alert!

Scholarship scam artists are the evil side of the scholarship industry. These folks lurk online or in hidden offices, spewing their phony offers to unsuspecting students. According to the Federal Trade Commission, examples of suspicious behavior include:

- Sending you "award announcements" for contests you never entered
- Claiming "guaranteed results" to bring you scholarship money
- Forcing you to pay "up-front fees" for generic scholarship lists
- Using language that sounds like the agents are government representatives
- Promising to deliver "secret scholarships" that no one else knows about

It's all bogus.

Another group of scammers are people who pretend to operate their own scholarship programs just to gain your personal information. With identity theft on the rise, be very careful.

I uncovered one of these folks while doing research for a local scholarship database. A guidance counselor called me to ask if I had ever heard of a particular scholarship. The application had a post office box, with no phone number, no website, no e-mail, and it requested students' social security numbers, their mothers' maiden names, and peculiar information about the applicants' childhoods. Unofficially, it had a high "stink factor" compared with the many high-quality, legitimate scholarships out there. Officially, my staff could not verify the scholarship or the identity of the supposed founder, and so we refused to post it to our website. Use your intuition, but also ask for an opinion at your school office or college's financial aid office if you suspect a scammer. The good news is that the overwhelming majority of individuals who work in the scholarship business are caring professionals who really want to help you.

To check out links on scholarship scam alerts, visit the www.scholarshipstreet.com website or visit the Federal Trade Commission website at www.ftc.gov for in-depth information on education and scholarship scams.

Breaking It Down

To be successful at finding scholarships, you should use four kinds of communication: online, print, word-of-mouth, and self-promotion. Online and print references should be used to verify each other. Word-of-mouth can be the most reliable, or least reliable, method of uncovering those hard-to-find scholarships. Self-promotion can border on bragging if done improperly. It makes people feel used to hear you talk about how great you are and then ask them for help. Self-promotion can also sound like entitlement, and scholarship judges do not like this approach. Remember, add a dose of humility. In this section you will learn how to use multiple methods for your scholarship search.

Let's get started. Refer to the scholarship tracking tool shown in figure 7–1. You can download a similar file from my website. The purpose of this tool is to organize and summarize the scholarships you find. For each scholarship that appears to be a match, enter the name, deadline, dollar amount, and source (where you found it). If your aunt Charlotte heard about it, then aunt Charlotte is your source. Keep this tool handy throughout your search, and be sure to read chapter 8 for help in ranking your scholarships.

Cyberspace Chase

Multiple websites boast billions in free cash for college. It seems so simple. Complete your profile, click the Submit button, and you will be matched to hundreds of scholarships. As you eagerly await the results, credit card companies, student loan guarantors, and athletic gear companies bombard your pupils with enticing ads. You can easily become distracted by all of the goodies and lose sight of your main purpose: to find free cash for college. As a reminder, the student loans they are offering you are not free. They are necessary sometimes to achieve your dream, but they are definitely not free.

| Name of the Scholarship | Initial Research | | | 1, 2, 3* | Application Materials | | | | | | | | | Competition | | Updates, Follow-up, Questions |
	Deadline	Amount	Source (person, website, book, etc)	RANK	Paper App	Online App	Essay	Letters of Rec.	Nomination Form	Transcript	Proof of Income Level	Samples of work	Other	# of applicants	# of awards	Comments

* Add symbols or colors to further indicate rank

Figure 7–1. Scholarship tracking tool.

Before you start your profile on the national scholarship search sites, place your scholarship worksheet next to you so that all of your academic and personal information is readily available.

As you complete the initial registration process, check every answer for accuracy. Scholarship search engines work on basic search principles combined with killer programming to give you back the list you want. Which site to use? Here's the inside scoop: Most national scholarship databases purchase their information from the same data warehouse. It's like ordering chicken at a restaurant—most of it comes from the same chicken suppliers, who package it under different names, sell it to food vendors, who sell it to restaurants, who sell it to you. They might add different spices, but it's still chicken. What does this mean for you? It means it is unnecessary to create a profile on every scholarship website. Choose two. Enter your profiles and see what you get. If you aren't happy, try a third.

If the sites are all similar, why do I suggest that you enter your profile in two or three? The answer is that you want to test their search capabilities. Although they have very similar information, they have different matching functions, just as Google and Yahoo are both search engines that use different methods for hunting the Internet. If I'm really looking for something obscure, I will try a third search engine, and sometimes that works.

Scholarships.com is one of the scholarship search sites that proactively collects firsthand updates from scholarship providers. The local scholarship websites I mentioned in this chapter also use the firsthand research approach to collect new information or verify existing information. Check out the case study about Kevin Ladd, the vice president of operations for Scholarships.com, to understand national scholarship databases better.

RESOLVE TO EVOLVE

Care to write an essay on the No Child Left Behind Act of 2001? How about the rising cost of a college education and what our government should do to offset the effects? No wimpy questions here. These topics are a part of the 2008 Resolve to Evolve essay scholarship, which is available to registered users of Scholarships.com. According to Kevin Ladd, a vice president at Scholarships.com, through this essay contest, the site

Kevin Ladd and his colleague Dan Walowski of Scholarships.com.

distributes $10,000 to seven students from the pool of applicants. Plus, you can search for other scholarships.

Much like other search sites, at Scholarships.com, you enter your personal and academic information and within seconds, maybe a minute tops, you receive a list of opportunities that match your profile. "We take the work out of the search," Mr. Ladd said. Ten years ago this level of accuracy and speed was unheard of in online scholarship searching. I won't get old-school on you, but you are really lucky. (Parents: Remember binders, books, and paper cuts? Hello!)

What sets Scholarships.com apart is that many scholarship search sites are populated by a generic database. Scholarships.com goes beyond the spoon-fed information and seeks out new information and updates from individual sponsors. So how can you, as a student, capitalize on these free resources? Be accurate, come back to change your profile, and pay attention. According to Mr. Ladd, it's easy for students who are eager and rushed to select the wrong categories. For example, users may select "college senior" instead of "high school senior," or accidentally hold the scroll function on the mouse, which will add erroneous information to the profile. As a *Scholarships 101* reader, you know to proofread your work carefully, so I doubt this will happen to you—it's just a friendly reminder.

Start early. Follow the rules. This is common advice, but Mr. Ladd sums it up nicely: "If you don't follow the rules, you run the risk of being automatically disqualified. Scholarship providers don't create 'Official Rules' to their scholarship for nothing. Those students who read the rules thoroughly and follow them to the letter will almost invariably have a considerable advantage." His other advice is to educate yourself about money so you understand basic finances when you go to college. He realizes the number of students relying on student loans is increasing. "Loans are, more often than not, a reality of college and students should educate themselves about the education loan process so they can get the best offer available to them."

Mr. Ladd sees a positive trend that should offer inspiration to scholarship-seeking students: Major corporations are entering or increasing their involvement in the scholarship field. "The students benefit from this venture and I hope the trend continues," he said.

Printed Publications

Newspaper readership has slowly dwindled in the past decade, especially among teens. Because most of your competition is *not* reading the paper, you might have an edge if you *start* reading the paper. Newspapers are a viable place to gather scholarship information because scholarship sponsors still send scholarship announcements to the newspaper hoping that your parents or grandparents will read it. The larger scholarship programs also purchase advertising space to announce their competitions, deadlines, and winners. Feature articles might describe an organization that is holding a scholarship fund-raiser. If an organization is raising money for scholarships, it is obviously going to distribute that money in the future. If you read about an upcoming scholarship banquet, it could mean two things: (1) an organization is honoring scholarship recipients, or (2) it is holding the banquet in order to raise money for a scholarship program. Once you start looking, you will find these events covered in the newspaper.

If your local newspaper has an online searchable archive, this is another place to retrieve information on scholarships. Technically, the scholarship announcement may have first appeared in print but is now available to anyone with a computer and an Internet connection. If you live in a city with a small, local newspaper, check out back copies at the library or search the online archive for dates near graduation time. This is most likely May or June of the previous school year. You might be able to find a listing of students who won scholarships last year, along with the names of the scholarships and the dollar amounts. It's a bit of digging, but you might uncover a gold mine of prospective scholarships.

Who is on your Team of Champions and who agreed to help you find scholarships? Grandparents are the perfect people to help you find possible scholarships by scouring the paper. Aunts, uncles, anyone else? If you don't subscribe to the newspaper, find someone else who does or make a weekly stop at the library to review its copies of newspapers.

Other printed sources of information, although my least favorite, are the huge scholarship directories available at libraries and at bookstores. I hesitate to use these because they are cumbersome and because technology-based search tools have far surpassed the functionality of these monolithic books. With luck, the directory will at least have a CD-ROM to expedite your search.

One reason to consult these directories, however, is that your competition probably isn't! Everyone's online looking for the fast fix on scholarships. Another reason to consult these larger directories is for state-based grants and financial aid or for a condensed version of scholarships in a particular field such as nursing, engineering, visual arts, etc. Keep track of where you find your scholarship information, and if you notice duplication between what you uncover in these books and your online searches, use them to verify each other. Does the contact information in the book differ from the scholarship database? If so, note the difference and verify the correct version by calling or e-mailing the sponsor to get the most current information. You can also quickly type the sponsoring organization's name into an online search engine and see if the sponsor has a website with the most current information.

The Auntie-Net

Former Secretary of State Colin Powell has a joke about the auntie-net being faster than the Internet. Believe me, if there's news in my family, the auntie-net wins. Faster than you can text message and hit "send," my aunts can spread the lowdown on what's what in the family tree. Harness the power of word-of-mouth advertising to bring you scholarship leads.

Who on your Team of Champions is connected to the most people? Who is an information junkie? Who always seems to know which stores have something on sale? Which new restaurants opened recently? These are the people who have their radars on "receive" when it comes to information gathering. Of course, it's no fun to gather all that information if they can't tell someone about it. If you put the word out to these folks that you are looking for scholarships—you *will* hear back.

When you do hear back, be sure to thank them, regardless of whether you decide to apply for that particular scholarship. The beauty of word-of-mouth advertising is the quickness with which information moves, but the drawback is inaccuracy. Remember that game when you were a kid where you whisper something into one person's ear and then ten people later it comes back to you as a distorted version of your original sentence? That could happen in your search for scholarships, so take the time to verify the information.

When I was looking for scholarship information to create a scholarship database in Wisconsin, my colleagues and I had research leads that turned out to be true and others that had magically morphed along the word-of-mouth information highway. For example, did you know that there is a scholarship competition for writing an essay on the value of fire sprinklers? It's true. When someone told me about it I thought, "Can this be real?" After investigating, I found out it was real. In another example, I heard that there were scholarships for children whose parents were in jail. A noble group decided that these children should not suffer because of what there parents had done. It turned out to be not so true! Okay, there were a few small local scholarships, but you had to be a member of their mentoring programs in order to qualify for assistance. The Center for Children of Incarcerated Parents does *not* have a scholarship.

It takes some digging to verify word-of-mouth leads, but it's an important part of your strategy. Never discourage someone who tells you about a scholarship he or she "heard about." Nod politely, thank the person, note the information, and investigate on your own. Oh yeah, if it turns out to be true and you apply for that scholarship, thank the person again!

Pick Me! Pick Me!

Self-promotion is the fourth method and most difficult part of your scholarship search because you want to impress people without alienating them. What is self-promotion? It's the craft of making sure that your name and your fabulousness is firmly planted in the minds of people who can affect your scholarship success. During the scholarship-search process, your self-promotion is subtle and it includes distributing your scholarship worksheet to people of influence who can help you. It also means taking time to highlight or point out your most distinguishing characteristics.

Simply introducing yourself and mentioning your quest for scholarships is an act of self-promotion. Don't go overboard telling people how great you are. Letters of recommendation are an example of the nuances of self-promotion that I will cover in chapter 8.

Special Circumstances

One of the hardest parts of my job is trying to help students who can't divulge information that could lead them to scholarships. These students may secretly search online or scan the headlines, but when it comes to self-promotion, they don't feel chatty about their personal pain. This is certainly understandable.

These students are bright enough to attend college but suffer tremendous setbacks on the road to enrollment. This section is for folks who need advice on special programs and scholarships available to students in unique situations.

If you face family circumstances, personal attributes, physical or emotional challenges, or other obstacles that are threatening your ability to attend college and gain financial aid, you should read this section. You might be tempted to skip it if you do not identify with one of the groups described in the following list. But I urge you to read this section because I am sure you know *one* person who could benefit. Pass it along, please.

The national scholarship databases include some of these scholarship categories, but probably not the small, local scholarships associated with them. Internet search engines may help you uncover the more obscure scholarships, or you may want to contact the support organizations related to these issues.

If you do not fall into one of these categories but have another personal situation, this advice will still help you refine your scholarship-search skills for whatever your personal issue might be. The section is organized alphabetically.

■ **Alcoholism and Alcohol, Tobacco, and Other Drug Abuse (ATODA) Prevention.** There are two types of scholarships in this category: those focusing on young people and adults in the recovery phase, and those focused on prevention.

Al-Anon, the organization for teens affected by alcoholism, does not offer scholarships at a national level, however, local chapters and affiliate programs may do so voluntarily. The best source of information is local, especially due to the confidential nature of these groups. One well-known fund is at Texas Tech's Center for the Study of Addiction and Recovery. To date, this is the largest campus-based scholarship program for students who are in recovery. A $1 million endowment was established to ensure the future of the scholarship program, but you must attend Texas Tech. Check your prospective college to see if it has something similar, although it's probably less than $1 million!

Another angle for scholarships in this category is to enter essay contests where the topic is the prevention of alcohol, tobacco, and other drug abuse. Have you heard of Drug Awareness and Resistance Education, otherwise known as DARE? It offers a scholarship. Local newspapers, community centers, schools, and government agencies are common sponsors. These types of scholarships lean toward essay contests.

■ **Cancer.** If you have survived cancer, are the child of a cancer survivor, lost a parent to cancer, helped take care of your siblings during a parent's cancer treatment, or endured cancer-related hardships in your immediate family, you may be eligible to apply for scholarships because of your experience. Cancer groups recognize not only the emotional and physical tolls of cancer but the financial devastation that can occur from medical bills. Scholarship sponsors range from local organizations that memorialize loved ones to national programs that seek to accelerate research about cancer prevention or to support students entering the oncology field. Many of the American Cancer Society's state and regional chapters offer Youth Survivor College Scholarships. Visit www.cancer.org to start. Other disease-related organizations offer scholarships, too, and you should follow similar methods to uncover them.

■ **Disabilities.** Scholarship sponsors have contributed funds to help students with physical, developmental, and learning disabilities. These funds are generally administered by a membership organization or association, but the money could also be in the pool of institutional funds at your college. Ask the transition specialist at your high school about scholarships for students with your disability, and consult with the disability-services coordinator at your prospective college. Financial aid can be used for disability-related expenses for your education, but it cannot be used if those expenses are already covered by a supporting agency. The college you attend must make accommodations and reasonable modifications for you to succeed. Whether you are deaf, have Asperger's syndrome, or have a learning disability, you can find scholarships to help pay for college. Start with the organization most noted for research or advocacy for your disability, then research national databases.

■ **Foster Children.** More than half a million children are in foster care in the United States, and I'm guessing some of them want to go to college. When foster students "age out" of the foster-care system, they face multiple barriers to enrolling in college and oftentimes have little support. The National Foster Care Coalition, the Orphan Foundation of America, and the U.S. Department of Health and Human Services provide various levels of information and support to college-bound foster students. Most noteworthy is a $5,000 voucher for foster children to continue their education after high school. This voucher is managed at the state level, and it is important for foster students and foster parents to ask their social workers or guidance counselors about it. The Orphan Foundation of America (www.orphan.org) is a great place to start. In addition to scholarships, it distributes care packages to college students who came from foster care.

■ **Lesbian, Gay, Bisexual, and Transgender (LGBT) Support.** Students who are lesbian, gay, bisexual, or transgender and are seeking scholarships may face additional hurdles if their sexual orientation is not accepted by their families or school communities. Although you can find information on LGBT scholarships in the national databases, it may be harder to uncover local scholarships if you haven't come out yet and are not connected to LGBT resources in your community. The Point Foundation offers merit-based scholarships for LGBT students who lack family support on the pathway to college. They also provide mentoring and leadership support to their scholars. The website is www.pointfoundation.org.

■ **Mental Illness.** Anxiety, depression, bulimia: You read about these subjects in the headlines, most likely after a tragedy. The National Alliance on Mental Illness (NAMI) is a hub of information for college-bound students and their parents. The NAMI website, www.nami.org, has a list of scholarship tips and campus affiliates, but like other scholarships, you are more likely to find sources locally. The NAMI chapter in your state or city is one place to start. The transition to college is a huge life change and can aggravate any existing condition you may have. Besides looking for scholarships, visit NAMI to gather advice and resources to ease your transition.

■ **Raised by a Single Parent or You are a Teen Parent.** Half of all marriages end in divorce, and a good portion of them leave children in single-parent households. Certainly, some single parents never married, but both situations can leave college-bound students in need of extra support. If you are a single parent or you are being raised by a single parent, help is available but can be hard to find. Sometimes these scholarships offer more than tuition assistance. Examples are day care grants, support groups, and parenting classes. The simplest scholarships help pay the cost of your college education, although the holistic programs will require a larger commitment from you and come with more support from the sponsor or the college.

If you are a woman who is a single parent, it is helpful to search sites for scholarships devoted to women. In my hometown, I am aware of two scholarships created by organizations for single parents and another one sponsored by a college. All three have different criteria and various levels of competition. At the national level, the Jeannette Rankin Foundation provides funds for single moms over the age of 35 who are returning to school. The Raise the Nation Foundation provides scholarships for single parents and the children of single parents who want to attend college.

■ **Undocumented Students or Youth Whose Parents are Undocumented (Sometimes Called Illegal Immigrants).** As the debate rages on about access to college for undocumented students, it is hard to quantify what financial aid is available for these students. Federal and state governments have conflicting policies, which can make it confusing for students and their parents (for whom English might be a second language).

The first differentiation is in whether or not you are a U.S. citizen. If you are a U.S. citizen, you have more opportunities available to you regardless of your parents' status. You can attend college like any other student as long as you can pay the bill. If you, like most students, need financial aid, you must complete the FAFSA. The FAFSA requires social security numbers. Although you may have one, your parents may not. Technically, you can use zeros (000–00–0000) for your parents' social security numbers, but I understand that students in your situation are hesitant to do this.

If you are *not* a U.S. citizen but attended high school in America for at least three years and graduated, some states will allow you to attend state colleges for the price of state resident tuition. You are not eligible for federal student aid. The policies surrounding this issue are constantly changing, so you may try to focus your efforts on private scholarship money instead. Private scholarship sponsors can designate whether you must be a U.S. citizen to qualify for their awards. If you are a U.S. citizen, you have every right to apply. If you are not, then you can only apply for scholarships that do not require citizenship. Some scholarship applications don't ask. There is also pending legislation titled the Development, Relief, and Education for Alien Minors Act of 2003 (the DREAM Act) that, if passed, would help you go to college. Two organizations that provide additional information are National

Council of La Raza (www.nclr.org) and the Mexican American Legal Defense and Educational Fund at (www.maldef.org).

■ **Other Struggles.** As you begin to think about your own struggles, look to supporting organizations for scholarship information. They may use terms like *financial aid, tuition aid, essay contest,* or *college opportunity* to describe what is essentially a scholarship. Many support organizations also offer scholarships to attend their annual conferences or to join their membership programs.

Scholarship-Search Pledge

The Scholarship Lady is asking a favor. Before you complete one scholarship application, please finish your scholarship worksheet. I know it's tempting to start your scholarship search with a few clicks in your browser, but if you don't have all of your information handy, how will you know what you are looking for? Picture a clearance-sale rack at your favorite store after a few million people have already stopped by. Not pretty. Nothing is in order. You don't really need those $2.99 flip-flops, but you got distracted by the neon sticker. The same thing will happen in your search for scholarships if you're unprepared and decide to "just browse." Make a pledge to yourself to be prepared and focused as you move ahead.

Fridge Notes

The search is on.

- **Cyberspace Chase.** What's your favorite scholarship search site?

  www. _____

- **Printed Publications.** Local newspaper? School newsletter? Start skimming for scholarships.

  _____

  _____

  _____

  _____

- **The Auntie-Net.** Who's the information maven in your family?

  _____

  _____

- **Self-Promotion.** Who knows about you and your quest for scholarship dollars?

  _____

  _____

- **Special Circumstances.** Identify any special issues you are facing and seek scholarships under those categories.

  _____

  _____

  _____

Chapter 8

Apply Now!

Y ou've accomplished a lot and it's time to acknowledge your work. You've assembled a Team of Champions, you have a dream and a plan, you created a scholarship worksheet and résumé, and you have a scholarship-search tool to document your research. All of your materials are neatly organized in your folder, right? Your Team of Champions, guidance counselors, family, and friends all know you are seeking scholarships, right?

Great! It's time to move on.

Until now we've focused heavily on scholarships, which makes sense because you are reading the book *Scholarships 101*. To give you a competitive edge, I'd like to share the basics of marketing and fund-raising and ask you to incorporate these ideas, where appropriate, into your scholarship strategy.

Applying for scholarships is similar to applying for grants— something I did professionally for more than a decade. I started my career working at an advertising agency, and after that moved into the nonprofit side of business. I helped educational organizations raise money to support their programs. This required me to write letters, fill out applications, write proposals, and ask people, foundations, corporations, and government agencies to "support our cause." We were usually asking for money, free services, or volunteer time. You, as a scholarship seeker, will follow a similar process.

Fund-Raising 101

Imagine someone walking up to you on the street and asking you for some money. How would that make you feel? You don't even know this person. Should you be charitable and hand the person some change or walk away as fast as you can? That's up to you, but in the world of scholarships, sponsors want to know something about you before they dole out their money or their time. The same goes for your helpers and Team of Champions. People will believe in you if you give them something to believe in. In fund-raising we rarely asked people for funding if we didn't have a relationship with them first. It's a breach of common courtesy to shake hands and then ask them to take out their checkbooks. In the world of scholarships, you have one advantage: People are willingly asking you to apply for their money!

What can you learn from the other students in this book? How did they approach the scholarship process? What basic themes come across in all of the profiles?

One basic rule of fund-raising is that you should never apply for money if you don't meet the criteria. It's a waste of your time and the donors' time, because someone who *does* meet the criteria is likely to apply. The same is true for scholarships.

Another reality of fund-raising is that people want to know they are making sound investments. They want to know that you will not squander the money they gave you. They want to be assured that you are honest, and most important, they want you to succeed. As you complete your scholarship applications, think, "Have I given them any reason to doubt me?" "Have I proved that I am a good candidate?" "Is it clear that I am a successful person who is likely to succeed in college?"

Fund-raisers use terminology similar to the sales profession. They have *leads*, *prospects*, and *priorities*.

A *lead* is a piece of information or profile about someone who *might* be a good match for an organization, but more research is required. It could be a lead on a new volunteer, a new board member, or a new donor. For you, scholarship leads are the information you gather through your scholarship search, whether you found the lead online, in print, or through word-of-mouth. You must follow up on that lead to find more information.

In the realm of fund-raising, a *prospect* is a solid lead—someone who has an affinity for giving to similar organizations. Prospects are looking for organizations like us and we are looking for donors like them. They have the ability and desire to help and we have a need aligned with their preferences. We have analyzed this prospect and determined that the organization is a good match. As you begin to review all of the scholarship information you collect, narrow down your list of leads by asking yourself, "Are they looking for people like me? Do their preferences match my profile? What is my likelihood of success? Is the dollar amount worth the effort to me?" Your answers will guide you in figuring out which scholarships are prospects for you. Your scholarship list becomes a viable roster of possibilities.

A *priority* is a prospect that has a deadline approaching or requires time to complete the necessary steps. There is urgency in responding to the priority. On your list of scholarship prospects, those that are due soon are your top priorities. Scholarships that require extra time for essays, letters of recommendation, and such will be priorities because you need to give your helpers sufficient time to respond.

To help you understand what motivates people to give away money, I'm going to ask you to pretend that you have $5,000 in scholarship money to give away and you cannot give it to someone in your family. How would you design the application process? How would students apply? What kinds of things would motivate you? Would you only want to give it to the highest-achieving students? To students who are needy? To students who went to your same high school? What are your minimum expectations? What might annoy you about applicants? If you can put yourself in the sponsor's shoes, it might help you submit a better application. So far, *Scholarships 101* has centered on you. Now I am asking you to think like the sponsor.

Another rule of fund-raising is that most of your money comes from a few sources who contribute a lot, and the rest comes from many smaller donations. This was true for a few of the students in this book. They received major, four-year scholarships from the colleges they attended and the rest were small amounts from other sponsors. The jackpot of the scholarship world are the four-year full-ride scholarships awarded by colleges to the students they really want on their campuses. A few national programs offer these long-term generous commitments, and they are very competitive. If you are a high-achieving student, you should invest a significant portion of your time in pursuit of these opportunities.

BEING A HUMANITARIAN PAYS OFF!

Combine a fear of student loan debt with a love for international travel and humanitarian causes and what do you get? A successful scholarship winner.

Courtney attended a large Catholic high school and her parents absolutely expected her to go to college. They started looking at colleges in sophomore and junior years but didn't know how they could afford a bachelor's degree and the master's degree Courtney planned to pursue.

"A lot of kids I went to school with didn't have a problem taking out huge loans but I didn't want to do that if I was going to graduate school, too. I didn't want to owe $125,000 in debt," she said.

Courtney plans to become a doctor or medical researcher, and she has a passion for international politics. She took advantage of the People to People Student Ambassador program, where she took two trips to Washington, D.C., two trips to western Europe, and two trips to eastern Europe. She also attended a youth humanitarian forum, which included a visit to Russia. She used her academic profile, school interests, and international experiences to set herself apart "from what average high school students would have under their belt."

Like many students, Courtney started in her guidance department and also used fastweb.com. "The school scholarship bulletins worked better for me because on the Web you are competing with so many people." She applied for fifteen scholarships and won six of them. She was also offered, and accepted, $12,000 a year for four years from the private college she chose to attend. Her application to the school was the only application required for the college's scholarships. She will offset the cost of college with more than $65,000 in someone else's money!

What other techniques did she use? She looked at the websites of organizations specific to her interests. Courtney said her mom helped track these down by searching the Internet. Courtney liked tennis and found the U.S. Tennis Association Tennis and Educational Foundation online. She applied for its scholarship and won.

Courtney also admits that she "made friends" with the person in her school office who handled scholarships *and* transcripts. Her advice is to plan ahead so the people who can help you have enough time for paperwork, proofreading, or letters of recommendation.

What's Courtney's advice to scholarship-seeking students? "Start earlier. The summer before senior year would be a great time."

What about the rest of you who weren't the valedictorian? You still have a tremendous shot because not all scholarships are designated for valedictorians. Your job is to be creative and invest in other "wow" factors that appeal to judges. Judges want to get to know you. You may have a unique, compelling story to tell; you may have overcome the odds; and you may offer a type of diversity to the talent pool that they are seeking. You need to position yourself in a way that makes you stand out from the competition.

You should also understand that judges try to use an objective process but they are human and they have emotions. I do not recommend overt emotional appeals. Judges do not want to read sob stories or fabricated tales of woe; however, a little well-placed emotion goes a long way. Judges do want to know what you think and how you feel about yourself and the world around you.

Free Money for Freshmen

Scholarship funds for incoming freshmen are distributed in two ways at most campuses: as an all-inclusive process where your application to that school *is* your application for freshman scholarships, or, as a separate process with separate applications for freshman scholarships. Ask about this when you apply.

In the all-inclusive process you need to make every attempt to create a compelling reason for the college to consider you for a scholarship, because it is making scholarship judgments based on your college application and personal essay.

Colleges have pools of money that they distribute each year. They use this money to lure students to their schools. How you fit in the mix is often a behind-the-scenes process where the school looks at all of the applicants to determine who is different in which ways, who is the usual applicant, and who will lend diversity to the class. For instance, if an out-of-state school offers you a scholarship, it may be trying to diversify its incoming class geographically. If you are a highly talented artist and not enough art-focused students have applied to that college, that's a reason for that college to offer you a scholarship. You must learn to be true to yourself and who you are and realize that what makes you unique at one college will be standard at another.

If you want a college to offer you a scholarship, think about what you bring to the table compared with the school's usual applicants. For example, maybe most students from your high school apply to the same two or three colleges. Those colleges know that they will have a steady stream of students from those high schools, so your application might not look special. Consider applying to a different college that few people from your high school have ever attended. You might be surprised at what it offers you.

FANCY FOOTWORK

You've read about a few students who received major scholarships from their colleges when they were freshmen. I want to share one more story. Last year I met Melissa, a woman who wanted to play soccer in college and, of course, wanted to win a scholarship. Her strategy was to apply to a smaller state school that had her major, where she would stand out as a soccer player, as opposed to a Division I school, where she might not. Her strategy worked and she was awarded a scholarship. The incredible competition made a scholarship from a Division I school less likely for her. She made a choice, the right choice for her, and the college paid her tuition. Think about your choices of colleges and how that might affect your ability to secure financial aid.

Mastering donor relations is another facet of fund-raising that you should try to incorporate into your quest for scholarships. Quite simply, it means responding to their phone calls, e-mails, and letters promptly. It means keeping them up-to-date on what you are doing. It means sending them thank-you letters, attending their scholarship banquets, and doing anything else that shows how much you appreciate their choice to invest in you.

I attended the National Scholarship Providers Association conference in 2007. You can see me pictured below with a scholarship provider. One of my many conversations with sponsors focused on gratitude. Some programs have experienced great success in keeping in touch with their students, and the students serve as ambassadors and spokespeople for the scholarships. Other programs struggle just to maintain mailing addresses. Your job is to thank your sponsors and keep them informed of any changes that affect your relationship with them. For example, if you change from full-time to half-time status, they need to know that. It could affect your

The Scholarship Lady with Molly Smith of the Boettcher Foundation, an organization that provides scholarships to students in Colorado.

award. More simply, if you have a new e-mail address, they would probably like to know that, too.

Assessment 101

You've already done your research to uncover scholarship leads, and in the Fund-raising 101 section you learned about leads, prospects, and priorities. Now we will assess which of those leads are your best prospects; that is, the scholarships that you have the greatest likelihood of winning. They are your priorities. We are going to use your scholarship tracking tool to help you focus your time and resources.

On the left side of the scholarship tracking tool from Chapter 7, you listed the name of every scholarship, its deadline, dollar amount, and where you found it. On the sheet, there is a small box for ranking the scholarship according to these four criteria:

1 = You exceed the criteria, you *should* apply

2 = You meet the criteria, you *could* apply (but should you?)

3 = You are close, but it *would* require extra work on your GPA, test scores, volunteer work, etc.

4 = No match—don't waste your time. Most scholarships in the universe will be a "4"—*they are not a match for you* and you should not enter them on the scholarship tracking tool.

The next step is to determine how much work is involved in applying for each one.

Under the next few columns you will see required "application materials" such as paper application, online application, essay, letters of recommendation, nomination form, transcript, proof of income level, samples of work, and "other." For each item, put a check in the box if the scholarship packet requires those materials.

On the right side, assess your competition. Historically, how many applicants apply each year and how many scholarships are awarded? This might require a little more research to find the answer. Type in the answers on your tracking tool. Students who skip this step may have a warped sense of priorities because they let the dollar amount dictate their priorities. If you can't find it, leave it blank for now.

For example, if you ranked a scholarship a "2" (you *could* apply), you find that only ten people applied last year, and two scholarships are awarded, this scholarship is a high priority. Put a star next to it, highlight it, or use colored text in your scholarship tracking tool, whatever works for you. Do something that will indicate its level of importance. If you ranked a scholarship a "3" (you are close but it would but it would require a boost in your GPA, test scores, or volunteer work), 300 people applied last year, and only one scholarship is awarded, this is a lower priority. If you have a scholarship ranked a "1" (you *should* apply), 300 people applied last year, only one scholarship is awarded, and it only requires a nomination letter and short essay, this is a high priority. You might want to ask someone on your Team of Champions to help you.

Remember that the 1, 2, 3, and 4 rankings are related to your eligibility based on your scholarship search. Taking the extra step of *assessing* your competition by the numbers puts in perspective which opportunities you should pursue first. You can still apply for the lower priority scholarships, but they should not consume all of your time.

The purpose of this exercise is to assess which scholarships are your highest priority based on your competition, how much work is required, your likelihood of success, and the deadline. The tool creates an objective process before pursuing a scholarship. Thousands of students apply to online scholarship sweepstakes because they are easy, not realizing their odds of winning could be 1 in 10,000. I challenge you to think about your priorities and use your scholarship tracking tool before you apply to any scholarship.

Marketing 101

Students who win one scholarship might be talented or plain lucky, but students who win multiple scholarships have learned how to package themselves. They are masters of marketing.

In a rhetorical sense, you are trying to sell yourself to the scholarship sponsors. You want them to buy your product (you) instead of the others (your competition). You may have heard people say that it's important how you package yourself to colleges; this is also true for scholarships. If you learn the basics of marketing and apply them to your scholarship efforts, you will increase your chance of success.

The four traditional principles of marketing are product, price, promotion, and placement.

Product

Your "product" is your accomplishments. Everything about you is the total package. Your grade point average, activities, scholarship essay, application, letters of recommendation, and anything else you submit to the scholarship committee is a reflection of you. The committee has probably never met you, and the only information on which it can base its decision is what you submit to it. Make sure it is your best effort.

Price

In marketing, the price of a product is one factor that determines whether someone buys it. What price does a scholarship committee pay to read your application? Monetarily, nothing; however, if time is money then it *is* paying a price. Scholarship committees are usually volunteers, and their time is precious. Good scholarship applicants will submit a neat package with all of the requested materials. If your materials are out of order, something is missing, or you skipped part of the application, it will cost the scholarship committee extra time, and it may move on to the next student.

Promotion

Self-promotion is hard to manage for students who have been taught to be humble. However, students who win scholarships have learned how to promote themselves without the appearance of bragging. Does your guidance counselor know that you maintained a B average the whole year? Does your favorite teacher know that you work part-time, want to go to college, and need money to pay for it? The first thing to do is tell everyone you know that you want to go to college. Second, tell people you are willing to work hard at being ready for college and finding scholarships. That second step will make you stand out.

You must promote yourself to the people around you—usually adults—

who can help you find scholarships or write letters of recommendation. When you submit the scholarship application, you must be confident that your own words and other people's words convey why you should win the scholarship. If they don't know about you, then how can they help you?

Placement

Placement is the last piece of marketing. If you have a good product, a reasonable price, and excellent promotion but no one can *find* your product, then you have just failed at marketing. If you want to win scholarships, you must be in the right place at the right time. Where exactly is that? You want to be where the information is collected: the library, guidance department, youth ministry, scholarship websites, newspapers, etc. You want to be around other students who are going to college. You want to find every opportunity to learn about scholarships and apply for the ones that match your profile. You want your scholarship application to arrive at the proper address on time. If your application is late or you can't find it, how will you win the scholarship?

Mediocrity vs. Standing Out

I have met many scholarship judges and scholarship sponsors over the years, and they are looking for students who stand out. These dear, generous souls must endure so much mediocrity that I know if you submit a stellar application, you *will* stand out. It's not uncommon for scholarship judges to serve on more than one scholarship committee, so even if you weren't chosen for one scholarship, they might remember your name for another one. Give them something positive to remember.

Applications 101

Before going on a scholarship-application blitz, choose one scholarship to test your efforts. What if you decide to apply for a dozen scholarships, all at once, using the same letters of recommendation and similar essays only to realize none are successful? You have no opportunity to go back. Ouch. Try one. Based on that experience, try two more. Then, complete three more. This one-two-three method will give you time to hone your skills and get feedback from your helpers. Don't wait to hear back after each one. Keep applying, but do it in stages. You might rework your essay, get better letters of recommendation, increase your GPA, or have other improvements along the way.

Most application forms require the same types of information. If you completed your scholarship worksheet, you will have this handy. The applications want to know your contact information, academic achievements, grade point average, awards, activities, and community service. They might also ask for short answers to questions about your goals, leadership experiences, or family background. If they request financial information, be clear about what information they are seeking. Is it a copy of your parents' tax return? Do they want to know your family's EFC? Your financial information is not on your scholarship worksheet or résumé, because I'm sure you and your parents don't want that information floating around among your Team of Champions.

I know that you are paying attention, but it's worth sharing the top ten class rules for Applications 101:

> "The one thing we convey to students is that they should include every piece of information that gives us a portrait of their high school experience, *only once* on the application."
>
> —P. Ross, SPONSOR

> "I want to know what their goals are and I want them to share it if they had a glitch."
>
> —M. Kellner, SPONSOR

1. Plan ahead.

2. Be proactive and persistent.

3. Apply for scholarships only if you match the eligibility criteria.

4. Complete the application neatly and in the requested format.

5. Answer the questions.

6. Provide the additional materials the sponsor requested, in the proper format.

7. Copy, for your records, all of your submissions.

8. Submit your application by the deadline.

9. Thank the people who helped you.

10. Start again.

Believe me, if you follow these rules, you will beat out part of your competition because they won't follow these rules, especially number ten.

HOT TIP

Sleep on It

How can you change zzzzzs into cash? If you really want to set yourself apart from the competition, get some sleep. Why would I encourage you to sleep in the quest for scholarships? Because you cannot complete a high-quality, compelling proposal if you're yawning at the keyboard. The tiniest little mistakes such as a wrong zip code, transposed number, misspelling of the sponsor's name, and the like will not get you where you want to go. If you proofread your work when you are most alert, you will catch things you never could after three cans of energy drink and a night at the computer. I know; this has happened to me.

101

Recommendations 101

You must gather information about well-matched scholarships to fully understand how to approach your supporters for letters of recommendation.

Know *what* you are asking people to do before you ask them to do it. What do the sponsors expect to learn from the letter, and how does that translate into instructions for your recommenders? Should they return their letters to you? To your guidance office? To whom should the letter be addressed? Is it supposed to be sent in the mail with your application or submitted online? Note these details before you approach anyone for help.

Give your recommenders a copy of your scholarship worksheet and your scholarship résumé. Point out or highlight important points that they should address.

When people ask me to write letters of recommendation, I only agree if I really know them. I want to do a good job and I know it's going to take me one to two hours of work to create a compelling, personalized document that speaks to that student's or employee's accomplishments. I love it when people provide me with copies of their scholarship applications, their essays, scholarship worksheets or résumés, and the key points they'd like me to make. They may ask other people for other key points so that the recommenders don't repeat the same information. If they provide me with clear instructions and a deadline that is a few days before they really need it, I'm in recommender heaven.

Give folks ample time to respond. People get sick, lose e-mails, and simply forget. You need to account for that in your timeline. Although your top priority is to win that scholarship, remember that your recommender may have other priorities.

Choose your references carefully. Letters of recommendation are only as good as the people who write them. If references treat your letter with great care, know you well, and can speak convincingly of your accomplishments and chance for success, you have struck gold. If you already know that the recommender cuts and pastes names into a generic letter used for every student, my advice is to find someone else to write your letter or provide the person with a draft of key information you'd like the person to consider when writing your letter.

Put yourself in your recommender's shoes. How well does the person know you? Is the reference willing to put his or her name and credibility on the line for you? Is he or she one of your biggest fans, or is the person your uncle's friend who happens to be the mayor of your town but doesn't know you? Scholarship judges do not want letters from elected officials unless those people know you well or unless a letter from an elected official is part of the nomination process.

If you do not have any rapport with your teachers or counselors, it will be difficult to stop them and ask for this favor, and the letter may suffer. I say "may" because it is possible to establish rapport quickly, and the person might know more about you than you think. Teachers talk.

Your school may have an established process for requesting letters of recommendation. I've seen excellent forms that students complete and submit to their recommenders, who then send the material back to the guidance office. Not every school has this process. Find out what the process is, if any, long before your first deadline.

A letter of recommendation is usually formatted with these key sections: introduction, how the person knows you, the recommender's impression of you, key points or facts about your accomplishments, how well-suited you are for that particular scholarship (if possible), your likelihood of success, an affirmation or recommendation for you, a thank you, and a closing.

Letter of Recommendation Format

1. Introduction
   a. The person's name and position and how the person knows you
2. Body
   a. The recommender's impression of you
   b. Specific examples and descriptive words
   c. Key accomplishments
   d. Your match to that scholarship
   e. Your likelihood of success in college
3. Closing
   a. The recommendation for support
   b. Thank you

Sample Letter of Recommendation

Dear Scholarship Committee,

Thank you for the opportunity to share my insights with you about Dominic Sinclair. I am a veteran teacher at Greenleaf High School. I've known Dominic for two years as his English teacher and newspaper advisor. Based on your criteria, Dominic is an excellent candidate for the Leadership All-Stars Scholarship.

Although we hold high expectations for all of our students, Dominic surpasses these expectations on a regular basis. For example, when the school newspaper staff agreed to submit issues for a national competition, it was Dominic who led his peers in organizing the effort. Through Dominic's leadership Greenleaf High School secured its first-ever award for school journalism. In the classroom, he is equally motivating to the other students and often propels our discussion to a new level with his earnest, investigative style of learning. You can see from Dominic's transcript that he has taken progressively more challenging courses during his four years here at Greenleaf. In addition to his academic accomplishments, I know that Dominic also produces an online journal in his spare time and has helped create brochures for community organizations.

I understand that character and leadership are the cornerstones of your scholarship. Dominic has proved in and out of school that he is trustworthy, caring, and conscientious. For example, his peers voted him "Citizen of the Year" two years in a row. Based on all of my interactions with Dominic, I foresee him doing very well in college and continuing his role as a student leader. He has the fortitude and perseverance necessary to excel on a college campus.

I highly recommend Dominic Sinclair for the Leadership All-Stars Scholarship based on his ability, character, and leadership. Thank you for your consideration.

Sincerely,

Ms. Casey

HOT TIP

Language Matters

What if I said, "Dominic is a hardworking student who is respected by his peers."? Too cliché! You should ask multiple people for recommendation letters so you can choose the best.

101

How long should the letter be? That depends on the sponsors. They may limit the letters to one page or "less than 500 words." The sponsor might have a nomination sheet that looks more like a form than a letter. It could be an online process. Basically, you need to provide whatever length and format the sponsor requires, which is why you want to be prepared before you ask anyone for a letter of recommendation.

After you receive letters of recommendation, make photocopies. If possible, ask for electronic copies so that you can easily modify the letters, with permission of course, and reuse them on other applications.

INSIDE THE MIND OF A SPONSOR

Mary Kellner of the Kelben Foundation manages a scholarship program that targets public school students. She came to our meeting with a six-inch-thick folder filled with scholarship applications. She wanted to be prepared for our interview, she said. This is a woman on a mission. What motivates a person like Ms. Kellner and what can you learn from her?

Mary Kellner launched her scholarship program for charitable reasons. Her husband became very successful in his business, so for Christmas one year, their family started a scholarship fund.

The first year they awarded one scholarship for $500. The next year it was two scholarships for $500. Last year they distributed forty-seven scholarships ranging from $500 to $1,500 each. They received seventy-five applications. That's good news for applicants. Students who apply have a better than fifty/fifty chance of winning a scholarship!

Ms. Kellner and her team of volunteer judges objectively evaluate the scholarships, but judges notice different things. For one judge, it could be attendance, for another it may be the completeness of the application. Ms. Kellner wants the essay to be personal. "For me, I want to know about them. I'm not impressed when students just say, `I need it, I want it, I need it,' that doesn't tell me anything."

It's important to these judges that applicants contribute as volunteers to their communities or schools. "Volunteer work and helping others is important but if they have to work or babysit their siblings, we certainly take that into consideration, too," Ms. Kellner said.

Ms. Kellner also takes an active role in learning about potential scholarship recipients. She said that counselors are crucial to the scholarship process, but counselors are being cut in the schools she targets. As a result, students don't hear about scholarships. "If we are on the fence about someone, we call the guidance counselor and ask questions," Ms. Kellner said. "If it's the week before the deadline and I don't have a lot of applications, I make calls and do outreach to schools."

How can students impress Ms. Kellner and her judges? Produce neat applications, provide the correct number of references, and answer the questions honestly and accurately.

Ms. Kellner shared one of her pet peeves with me: "Students who don't change the name of the scholarship on their application. You can tell they cut and pasted the information." Ouch. If you want to win scholarships, at least make sure you put the right name on the application.

Essays 101

Essays are like music: there are different genres and beats, but they are predicated on core principles. Whether you are into punk rock, pop, country, hip-hop, or one of the hundreds of subgenres, you can tell the posers from the real thing. It's the same when scholarship sponsors read essays. They can tell a true voice from a phony voice, good grammar from poor grammar, and a solid premise from a shaky one. Every person I interviewed for this book, and every committee member I have served with, asks for the same thing: better essays. Even the students who won scholarships felt that they should have spent more time on their essays because they probably would have won more scholarships.

Core Essay Elements

Scholarship essays follow the same format as other essays, but the content falls into three categories, depending on what the sponsor asked you to do. Most scholarship essays are personal, expository, or persuasive. You will be asked to present your personal story, a body of knowledge, or a convincing argument. Look at the essay requirements carefully and determine what the sponsor is asking of you: personal experience, information, or persuasion? Then, build your common elements: the introduction, body, and conclusion. The introduction includes your thesis, the body includes your supporting paragraphs, and the conclusion is your summary. I know this is a basic format, and I only share it as a reminder. In scholarship essays the content is just as important as the quality of writing, and you have the benefit of letting judges get to know you.

The reason essays are important in the scholarship world is because essays provide the sponsors with insight into the accomplishments, challenges, and psyche of the student. In addition, if you can't write a coherent, one-page, persuasive essay, how well will you fare in college? Besides the transcripts and test scores, what else is it about you that would give sponsors reason to support you? Have you challenged yourself? Have you overcome challenges? What are you passionate about?

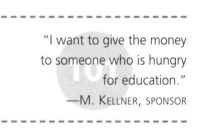

"I want to give the money to someone who is hungry for education."
—M. KELLNER, SPONSOR

Some sponsors require a specific theme for the essay, such as "tell us about your college goals" or "describe your philosophy of success." Others challenge you further and ask you to share your opinions on a political issue or personal obstacle that you overcame. Everyone has a story to tell. If you are not a good storyteller, you can brush up on these skills prior to writing your essay. Don't mistake "story" with the word fiction. You are telling a true story using all of your narrative skill and charm. The best stories are a combination of facts, anecdotes, and emotion. Personal stories make people feel happy, sad, concerned, motivated, etc. Good scholarship essays are informative *and* inspirational. They give the readers (judges) something to talk about. The judges are waiting, eagerly, to be wowed.

Essay Slam

In your quest for scholarships, I challenge you to the ultimate essay slam. I challenge you to become a fine-tuned essay-emitting machine. If you are headed for college, you should be enrolled in advanced composition classes in high school. These types of classes give you time to develop as a writer. The best way to improve your skills is to write more and open yourself to critique. I have yet to see a scholarship application that asks you to compute a mathematical formula (okay, maybe at the graduate school level!). Like it or not, writing matters.

In college-prep high schools, the college application and essay components are often built into the curriculum through class assignments. If you do not attend a school that requires you to devote time to these tasks, you need to carve out time to do it. One of the easiest ways is to use your class assignments as opportunities to write your college or scholarship essays, so that regardless of the scholarship essay topic the sponsor poses, you can respond in a coherent, well-crafted manner. This is what judges want. When it comes to the competition, your essay can put you over the top. Reference your dream if you need extra inspiration.

Despite overwhelming evidence of the need to invest in essay writing, not every student will *act* on this advice and *excel* in his or her efforts. If *you act* on this advice and *you excel* in your efforts, you will be far closer to scholarship success than your peers. If you choose to accept the challenge, you will be better prepared for college and more likely to submit high-quality, compelling scholarship applications.

> "This is not creative writing. This is 'tell us about yourself.' It should be genuine. Essays that start, 'if I were a tree,' aren't going to work for us."
> —J. McKenzie-Flynn, SCHOLARSHIP ADMINISTRATOR

In addition to in-class assignments, other ways that you can improve your essay-writing skills are to write practice essays based on common scholarship themes. You can also look ahead to scholarships that you might apply for and start working on the essay questions now. The beauty of this challenge is that you are in charge and you will set the parameters. If you want to get a little more creative, challenge some of your college-bound friends to join your essay slam, set a deadline, and read your work out loud. Share with one another what worked and what didn't. Think about how you can practice writing, in a fun way, to ultimately improve your essays.

> "Work at finding your voice. It's not simply about being organized. If it has a unique voice, tone, and sound, it begs for someone to read it."
> —C. Kelsey, TEACHER, ESSAY REVIEWER, AND AUTHOR

Active vs. Passive Voice

I never intended for this book to be a primer on English, but after completing my interviews, talking with teachers, and listening to participants at my boot camps, I realized some students need pointers on the craft of writing, which is different from the content of your writing. There's one huge caveat: I am not English teacher, but an author. Authors rely on editors and proofreaders, similar to your Team of Champions. Consult with your English teacher if you want specific exercises that can boost your essay-writing ability.

If you are heading off to college, I hope you know the difference between active and passive voice. If you do, you will excel beyond other students. If you still struggle with this, here's a down-to-earth definition I created that I'm sure will send English teachers into a tizzy: In active voice, you or the subject are doing something to someone or something. In passive voice, something is being done to you or to the subject, or worse yet, nothing is being done. Writers who repeatedly construct sentences without active verbs are giving their essays the kiss of death. They bore the reader. We all use passive voice occasionally, but the majority of your sentences should be active voice. Notice the difference in the following sentences:

PASSIVE: A 3.0 grade point average was received by me.

ACTIVE: I earned a 3.0 grade point average. (Much better, it shows that your 3.0 didn't magically appear, but you earned it!)

PASSIVE: I was nominated team captain and it was announced at the competition. (Who nominated you? Who announced it?)

ACTIVE: My teammates nominated me for team captain and our advisor announced it at the competition.

PASSIVE: I was awarded $5,000 from the Charles Fund.

ACTIVE: The Charles Fund awarded me its top scholarship of $5,000.

Remember, the scholarship judges don't know you, so you need to take every opportunity to make a positive impression. Writing with active sentences is one way to do it. I check myself by using the grammar tool in my word processor. If I see more than 10 percent passive sentences, I go back and edit my work. Try it.

Recycling

In your quest for scholarships, you will save time by using a slightly modified version of your perfectly crafted essay for multiple scholarship applications. This is honest, acceptable, and common in the scholarship world. It's called "personalizing your pitch" and it is a valuable, efficient method. Personalizing your pitch means that you take a general format or body of information and tailor it to fit the needs of your audience. Proofreading your work is doubly important if you do this because you don't want to leave information from the last scholarship essay in your current scholarship essay. This is the most common and easily correctible mistake I see on student essays. An extra round of proofreading, by someone other than you, can catch this error.

I strongly caution you against recycling a *generic* essay, because judges do not want to read generic essays in an original or modified form. Your attempt at recycling may turn into regurgitating because it's easier . . . but frankly, it tastes bad.

Think about it this way: if you create one generic essay and modify it for each sponsor, then all of your essays are based on generic writing. It's like generic essay offspring. Start from an impeccable, compelling essay and use the best parts to create a meaningful essay for each potential sponsor. I'll buy generics at the grocery store, but I'm not buying it in an essay.

Illegal Recycling

Recycling your own work is fine; recycling someone else's work is called plagiarism. It's easy to download a "sample" essay from the Internet, but if you submit that essay to a scholarship sponsor, you are seriously jeopardizing your academic future. You could be caught and then suspended or expelled from school, and your future colleges could be alerted to your actions. Besides that, what's the Fabulous Factor of an essay that thousands of other students could be using? How could it possibly be unique? Your best stories are your own true stories.

My advice to prudent students who seek to save time and have a positive impact on the judges is to use an a la carte approach. Look at your essays and pull out key phrases—the golden ones that are perfectly crafted and tell your story well. Look at the paragraphs that are essential and will set you apart from the competition. Those are the ones that you want to reuse. Ask someone on your Team of Champions to help you with this if it's hard to critique your own work. Think, too, about reusing an essay just because it was successful on one application. Your essay may have been perfectly crafted for that sponsor or that topic but could be ineffective for others.

Persistence 101

You learned that a combination of talent, preparation, persistence, and luck could contribute to your scholarship success. We agreed to leave luck in the dust. You have talent and, after learning the basics of *Scholarships 101*, you are prepared. That leaves us with persistence! You must keep going if you want to win scholarships.

As you begin to use your tools, remember to be flexible and allow time for revisions. If you boosted your grade point average in the last marking period, make that change on your worksheet and résumé. Continue to search for new scholarships and evaluate your success with the first six scholarships. If you use all of the same information on the first six applications and you didn't win a scholarship, ask someone on your Team of Champions for a critique. Do you appear to be a worthy investment in the mind of a scholarship provider? Are you closely matched to the type of student sponsors are seeking? What were the odds of winning?

> "You have to continue to apply and not get frustrated knowing that you won't get the majority of them."
> —COURTNEY, SCHOLARSHIP WINNER

Continue to check all of your sources for new scholarship opportunities. I've seen the widest smiles from students who win one scholarship, and after they win once, the feeling is contagious. Make sure to tell your Team of Champions if you were successful. Remember those thank-you notes? It's time to dust off the note cards and envelopes, and whether you win or not, thank the people who helped you along the way.

Keep going. Dream, plan, act, and excel your way to scholarship success.

Fridge Notes

Applications 101

1. Use your scholarship tracking tool to prioritize your scholarship applications. Look at your leads. Which ones are good prospects? Which ones are top priorities?

   _____

   _____

   _____

   _____

   _____

   _____

2. Remember the principles of marketing: product (you), price (hassle-free), promotion (who knows about you?), and placement (where should you be?).

3. Write active rather than passive sentences. Use strong action verbs.

4. Choose the right people to submit letters of recommendation on your behalf, and provide them with the information they need to do the job well. List them here:

   _____

   _____

   _____

   _____

   _____

5. Invest in your essays. Craft personalized essays for each application, using your best sentences and paragraphs. Recycle carefully. Combine information and inspiration to create a compelling essay. Let judges "get to know you."

6. Proofread everything more than once. Ask someone else to proofread, too.

Chapter 9

The Next Round

W hat next? Once you submit your applications, whether online or in a paper format, it can take weeks or months to hear back. You may feel as if your whole life is on hold. Do not wait. Keep applying for scholarships.

Visit with your Team of Champions. Keep your helpers informed. Take a look at your essay one more time. Use the time to focus on your second-priority scholarships and to revisit some of your original sources. Remember to update your profile in the online scholarship databases. Haven't been to the library in a while? Stop in and see if it has any new resources.

Be sure to check your voice mail, e-mail, and snail mail on a daily basis. You might think these methods are for old people, but most scholarship judges will *not* alert you in a text message or an instant message. They are generally not cruising your social-networking websites—unless they are checking up on candidates! These are businesspeople and volunteers, and they use more traditional modes of communication. Only the most progressive are tied into the technology of seventeen-year-olds.

If you want the sponsors' money, you need to be responsive

to their requests. This could be a request to submit your latest report card, set up a phone interview, attend an in-person interview with the scholarship-review panel, or attend a banquet.

You Are a Finalist

The phone rings and your mom answers it. She starts jumping up and down and waves you over. "Yes, he's here," she says and hands the phone to you. You grab the phone and listen as a friendly but unfamiliar voice congratulates you on your wonderful scholarship application. "We are considering you for the scholarship but would like to meet you first. Can you attend an interview next Saturday?" This scenario means you've made it to the next round. Sponsors might call you a semifinalist.

Semifinalists are in scholarship limbo, which is a better place to be than the rejection pile. Semifinalists are the cream of the crop, the best of the applicants, the students who show promise of winning but must prove their scholarship worthiness in one more way. The most important thing to do at this stage is thank the sponsor for selecting you as a semifinalist and assure the person that you can be available for the interview or will provide whatever additional information he or she needs to make a decision. This good-news scenario can actually leave students with pits in their stomachs or sudden headaches. You could feel excited and fearful at the same time. Mostly, you should feel proud that you made it this far. Now it's time to bring your "A" game to the next level.

COCA-COLA BY THE NUMBERS

To understand every aspect of applying for a scholarship, it helps to ask the experts. Ms. Patti Ross is the vice president of programs at one of the largest scholarship programs in the country, Coca-Cola Scholars. She previously worked for thirteen years as a high school guidance counselor. I interviewed Ms. Ross to help you form a clear picture of the application process for the Coca-Cola Scholars program. Here's what I found out.

The Coca-Cola Scholars Foundation was created by Coca-Cola bottlers and The Coca-Cola Company in celebration of Coca-Cola's centennial. Twenty-five million dollars was raised to start the program. In 1989, it distributed $1.1 million to 150 students. In 2007, it distributed $3 million to 250 students.

More than 200,000 people visit the Coca-Cola Scholars website each year and about 40 percent of those complete an application—roughly 80,000 students. The next time you watch football think of New York's Giants Stadium or Texas A&M's Kyle Field, which each hold about 80,000 fans. Now imagine if every person in the stands applied for that scholarship!

After the first round, Coca-Cola narrows down the applicants, based on its criteria, to 2,100 semifinalists who represent ten regions of the United States. The regions are based on the number of bottlers in that area, demographics, and the number of high school graduates. The semifinalists are asked to submit another application.

A committee of thirty readers, composed of high school counselors and college-admissions advisors, meet in Atlanta to review the semifinalists' materials. The staff monitors this process but the staff does *not* read, review, or judge the applications. The readers (judges) review the applications in teams of three to increase the validity and reliability of the process, and there is always one veteran judge in the group (a person with at least three years' experience). Based on this review, the judges select 250 Coca-Cola Scholars.

These 250 students each participate in an interview. The results of the interview determine who will receive a $10,000 scholarship and who will receive a *Patti Ross of the Coca-Cola Scholars program.* $20,000 scholarship! Whew.

Respond in a timely manner to any requests from the sponsor. It is closely evaluating everything you do from this point forward. Your competition has also made it to the semifinalist stage. You do not want the sponsor to go back to the panel and say, "Well, he didn't seem that excited when I called him," or "She didn't sign the verification form on time." You want the sponsor to know that you are sincere, grateful, and serious about meeting *the sponsor's* needs. You want the sponsor to know that you are thrilled and enthused.

Interviewing 101

You can read countless articles on the Internet or in print about how to participate in an interview, but the best advice I've found can be summed up in three phrases: (1) do your homework, (2) be professional, and (3) practice aloud. Let's discuss each part.

Finalist Homework 101

When I say "do your homework," I'm not talking about calculus. I mean do your research about that scholarship. If it's a small, local sponsor, try to find articles about the organization or business. Go back to your original scholarship tracking tool and review the information you gathered. If it's a large organization or national scholarship, it might have alumni profiles or a company history on its website. It is important to know about the sponsor's values and motivation to help you frame your answers. (This is also good advice when you apply for a job.) For example, if you know that the company was started as a family business and your family operates a small business, you might mention that. Why? It shows that you understand the values upon which that company was founded and will help you make a connection. When I have a chance to interview and hire students for jobs or internships, I always ask them to tell me what they know about the organization. I have rarely hired students who say, "Uh, I really don't know much about your organization." On the other hand, if students show up with a basic knowledge about the organization and our goals, that shows me that they have more motivation than their competition and they cared enough to "do their homework."

If you are part of an interview process, you also want to know about your audience. It is perfectly acceptable to ask questions if you are not clear about the audience and the format. Will it be a fifteen-minute interview or one hour? Will it be with one person or a panel of judges? Is there anything special you can do to prepare for the interview?

If the sponsor has been conducting interviews each year for ten years, it will probably have a set format and will provide you with detailed information. If the scholarship is new, the sponsor might not have concrete answers for you because the process is new to it, too. It's okay to ask.

Professionalism 101

What does it mean to "be professional"? It means that you show up for the interview on time, dress neatly, use proper English, avoid slang, and look people in the eye when you talk to them. You shake hands and say please and thank you. I won't give you an etiquette lesson, but I will encourage you to think about how people perceive you.

Maybe you made it to the semifinals because you are a stellar student who is a really good writer, but if the scholarship provider has an alumni program or expects you to be a spokesperson as part of your role as scholarship recipient, that person wants a chance to meet you. If you are going to represent the sponsor's business or organization and it dubs you as its "scholar" on your college campus, the sponsor wants to make sure that you don't show up in lederhosen. Unless, of course, it's a folk-dancing scholarship. In the simplest of terms, sponsors want to get to know you better.

Part of being professional is acting like a young adult who is destined for greatness—the type of young adult that sponsors can trust to go to college and graduate. You want to be confident, but not cocky.

Practice, Practice, Practice

Practicing interview scenarios aloud is a good way to squelch your nervousness and polish your public speaking. Early in my career, a co-worker suggested that I record myself when preparing to give a presentation. It was his polite way of letting me know that I relied on the word *um* anytime I needed a pause (about one hundred times too many) and that I had a penchant for the word *whatnot*. *Um* is not a word, and *whatnot* is not meant to be abused. They were distracting to anyone who had to listen to me for more than five minutes. Scholarship committees do not expect college-bound students to be professional public speakers, but they do expect college-bound students to be able to start and complete coherent thoughts in an articulate manner. The more you practice, the better you will sound.

You might feel uncomfortable with the concept of role-playing or acting out your interview. I know that when done poorly role-playing feels contrived and hokey. When done properly, it can provide invaluable practice at what you will say and how you will say it. If you have enough time before the scholarship interview to set up a mock interview, I strongly encourage you to do this. Ask a friend or family member to simply ask you a potential question and allow you to respond. That person is not to interrupt you and should only provide feedback when you are done. Listen to the feedback and adjust your speaking style as needed. Are you talking too fast? Are you relying on *um* to get you from one sentence to the next? Are you delivering boring, one-sentence answers or brilliant, insightful responses? If you must practice alone, that's okay, too, but try to critique yourself.

> "Assuming students have a good sense of self-awareness, they know which characteristics have enabled them to be successful. Find a way, during the interview, to share that information with the committee. There are generally enough questions in the interview that students can find a way to fit in that information and still stay on track."
> —P. ROSS, SPONSOR

It is common for scholarship committees to ask you about your application or to repeat one of the questions you already answered on the application. Before you go to an interview, review what you already told them. Look at the photocopy of the application you submitted (good thing you made a copy). Is there something you wish you would have said that you didn't? Mention that in the interview, if time allows. The simple act of reading your scholarship-application answers aloud is one way to prepare for the interview. Think about your audience. What else might it want to know about you?

Examples of Questions. Scholarship sponsors want to meet you so they can see the face behind the name. Who is this wonderful, fabulous, talented student who wrote a convincing essay? Are you a good match for their scholarships? If you are not sure where to start in preparing for your interview, try answering these practice questions aloud. You might want to type your answers first, but don't bring the typed answers into the interview room.

Bring your ideas and true self, and don't forget to answer the questions they ask you. Rambling is not an answer.

- **"What are your plans for college?"** (Be specific and emphasize that you will earn a degree rather than just go to college to escape your parents' house.)

- **"Why do you want to pursue that major?"** (Your answer is very important if the scholarship is designated for certain careers, interests, or majors; it's less important for general scholarships. If you are undecided about your major, you might want to share why, but be clear that you intend to earn a degree, not waste their money.)

- **"Tell us a little more about yourself."** (Caution: It might impress your friends that you can hit forty miles an hour downhill on your skateboard, but that's not what judges want to know. Keep your comments related to your academic, extracurricular, or family information.)

- **"We noticed from your essay that you have a passion for _____. Please elaborate on that."** (There's a fine line between being a fan and a fanatic. Clearly discuss your passion, but don't go overboard.)

- **"Where do you see yourself in ten years?"** (Frankly, I hate this question but it is so common in interviews. Regardless of my muttering about it, you should be prepared for this type of question.)

- **"Why are you the best candidate for this scholarship?"** (I love this question. This is your big chance to sell yourself to the committee members and convince them that you are the best investment they can make. Be enthusiastic and persuasive, and remember your dose of humility. Provide an emotional hook backed up by your facts. After everything you've learned in this book, you can do it!)

Remember, the judges want to get to know you. They don't want phony answers that you think they want to hear. They also don't want to be offended. Think carefully about this chance to win them over.

Logistics. On the day of the interview, who among your Team of Champions will drive you to the interview? Is there gas in the car? Will you drive yourself? Where should you park? Which entrance should you use? Are you going to take the bus or ride your bike? These little things can make a difference. You don't want to show up sweaty and nervous because you drove around the block six times looking for a parking space. If you are lucky, the committee will conduct the interview in an easily accessible place that is familiar to you—possibly at your high school.

What should you bring with you? Did the interviewer request extra materials? If you are going to an audition instead of an interview, what are the specific items or skills you need to be ready to showcase? Are the interviewers requesting your artist's portfolio or a miniperformance? Are you working on a new piece or will you present a classic? Which one will be the best artistic vehicle for your skills? Answer these questions well in advance of your interview or audition, and practice, practice, practice.

Passionate, Persistent, or Pushy?

Dear Parents,

I know it can be tempting to take over the scholarship-application process. If only your daughter had revised the essay, if only your son had worn a belt to the interview, if only you could control the process . . . and the list goes on.

Your role should be as a passionate fan and a persistent parent. Pushy parents annoy scholarship committees. Yes, you think your kid is fabulous and so do all of the other parents of the other kids who made it to the semifinals, but you must draw the line very clearly about what you can and should do for your child.

Scholarship judges are a savvy group of people and they know that you care deeply about your daughter or son, but you need to let your child "own" his or her pursuit of scholarships. Here are some ways you can support your future scholarship winner.

- **Designate "scholarship days."** On these days, your child is exempt from all chores as long as he or she is crafting scholarship applications. Your child must maintain his or her studies for school and maintain his or her participation in activities, but can someone else vacuum that day? Applying for scholarships is an extra time commitment. Be a hero and designate chore-free scholarship days!

- **Be realistic about what you know.** If you are not a good writer, then suggest that someone else proofread the essay for spelling and grammar; you only share your advice about the content. If you are a master at interviewing because you work in human resources, give your child a few pointers, but don't expect a seventeen-year-old student to interview like a forty-year-old professional. Help your child based on what you know.

- **Help conduct a mock interview.** Here's a twist: Team up with another college-bound family and switch kids. That way, you are not critiquing your own child and it might be more objective. You ask the other kid questions and the other kid's parents ask your kid some questions. The point is to practice answering the questions. You can become the Fantastic Four of interviewing.

- **Provide supplies and stamps.** In chapter 5, I asked students to set up their scholarship headquarters. This could be a nice little gift from you. If you know of a student who could use supplies or extra help, maybe you could pitch in for him or her, too. Yes, that's right, the Scholarship Lady gave you permission to go shopping!

- **Offer advice if you feel comfortable doing so.** Nudge students along, but don't nag them. Applying for scholarships can be stressful for everyone because the cost of college is such a burden on families. Think back to when you were seventeen. Did your parents expect you to raise $20,000 in the last semester of high school? Please, offer your child some comfort.

- **Celebrate accomplishments.** Whether it's a pat on the back, a hug, a phone call, or a pizza, make sure that you acknowledge the extra hard work that your child is doing to secure money for college.

- **Do an extra favor.** If you know of a kid who doesn't have parental support, help that kid. Please. You may be the sole member of his or her Team of Champions.

Lucky You

If you interview for more than one scholarship, then you have the luxury of improving your interview skills as you go along. Pay attention to your performance and the judges' responses during the interview. Note key phrases or ideas that pique the judges' interest or ones that cause them to pause or wrinkle their brows in confusion. Looking for these nonverbal cues is an essential way to gather information.

The committee is also interpreting your nonverbal cues. Keep distractions to a minimum. Fidgeting and squirming are signs of nervousness. If you practice ahead of time and are lucky enough to get multiple interviews, you will become more comfortable at interviewing. You will develop a clarity in your speaking that reflects focus and confidence—traits common in seasoned speakers.

Fridge Notes

Keep It Moving!

❏ Continue your search for scholarships.

❏ Update prospects and leads on your scholarship tracking tool.

❏ Check voice mail, e-mail, and snail mail on a regular basis.

❏ Provide any extra materials that sponsors requested.

Become an Interview Expert

❏ Practice your interviewing skills (greet people, make eye contact, focus your thoughts, pace your voice).

❏ Read your essay aloud.

❏ Use the practice questions or make up your own. Be prepared for the judges to ask whether you have any questions for them. What would you ask if given the chance? (Hint: Don't ask, "When do I get the money?" Ask something about the judges or the organization.)

❏ Pick out your clothes for the interview ahead of time. What will you wear if you are chosen for an interview?_____

_____

❏ Arrange transportation, if needed. How will you get to your interview? _____

_____

Techno Tools and Traps

I n your quest for scholarships, how much will you rely on
technology to assist you? Computers, cell phones, e-mails,
text messages, databases, online archives, websites, copy machines, search engines, and online forms are all possible tools of
a modern scholarship search, but are they necessary? If you try
to impress the sponsors by sharing your blog, podcast, or vod-
cast, will they know what that means and how to use it? Five
years after the publication of this book, will that technology and
terminology still be viable?

Let's take a look at how you can use technology to streamline the process, save time, and improve your odds of winning
scholarships.

Phone

First, you need a phone number that you can distribute to sponsors. Your phone number, preferably, will have voice mail capabilities. Why? So people can leave you messages. There is no need
for background music or a funny introduction in your voice
mail, just tell callers whom they've reached (to reassure them
that they dialed correctly) and ask them to leave a name and

number. Think about a potential scholarship sponsor and the impression you want to leave with that person.

E-Mail

Your e-mail address should be straightforward and should avoid any references to how hot or studly you are. Don't call yourself a geek either. Pick a clearly identifiable prefix (the part that goes before the @ sign) that won't make your mother blush. Why? Scholarship sponsors are professionals and volunteers, most of whom are older than you, and they don't need a daily dose of misspelled monikers like "delite" and "2hot." Remember, you are making a first impression. You can set up your e-mail account so that your professional-sounding e-mail name forwards to your usual e-mail account. Ask a tech-savvy friend to do this or use your e-mail program's "help" function if you don't know how to do this.

You can also use your e-mail to distribute your scholarship profile to your Team of Champions, distribute your essay for review, send friendly reminders to your recommenders, and serve as the communications hub for your fast-growing scholarship empire. You've probably heard it before, but take special care to proofread your e-mails before hitting that "send" button, and don't "reply to all" unless it's necessary.

If you never use your e-mail account—and I understand many students don't—you should promise yourself that you will check it once a day while you are applying for scholarships.

Networking and Sharing

YouTube, MySpace, Facebook, Yahoo 360, Helio, LinkedIn, Flickr, Photobucket—the names may change over the years, but the purpose is still the same: to connect you with people and share information around the globe or maybe around the block. What you can accomplish on the Internet today may be accomplished on your *phone* tomorrow, and it's hard for the adults around you to keep up (which could be the point, I know).

Although you might hang out online every night, very few scholarship sponsors are highly savvy about social-networking sites such as MySpace or Facebook and only a few have set up their own profiles. It's highly unlikely that the majority of scholarship providers will be chatting with you and your friends online, and I'm guessing that's fine by you.

Think carefully about whether people have information, videos, or pictures that relate to you, and remember that everyone is just one click away from millions of people through the power of technology. This is great if you are starting a new youth-led campaign to end violence and are building a base of supporters online, but it's not so great if your archenemy uploads a picture of you giving the bird to her camera phone (or something worse). No amount of backspacing and deleting can get rid of it. Although it's highly unlikely that a scholarship judge would see it, the chance is there. Don't risk it.

Never before has the ability to create and disseminate information been so disproportionate to the longevity of that information. In one minute or less you can leave a technological footprint that will outlive you.

"YOU SAID *WHAT* on MySpace?"

Students *and parents* should listen to Candice Kelsey. I am humbled by her qualifications as a school founder, a high school English teacher, an essay grader for the College Board's AP literature exam, an essay scorer for ACT, and a former consultant to the U.S. Department of Education. She also is the author of *Generation MySpace: Helping Your Teen Survive Online Adolescence*. Students, this is not another rag on MySpace; keep reading!

Ms. Kelsey wrote a book to bridge the generations and increase understanding about teens' online lives. What's her motivation? "As a teacher who devotes every day to helping students, I noticed that their online habits were standing in the way of their success and happiness," she said. "They were struggling with the drama caused by their online activity."

According to Ms. Kelsey, 68 percent of the college admissions officers and human resource officers she interviewed would make a decision whether to pursue a candidate based on their online profile. "It wasn't as much about what students published about themselves but the poor judgment they exercised by putting it online," she said. Scholarship sponsors and judges might feel the same way.

Even students who start their online lives for positive gains can become derailed. Ms. Kelsey shared the story of one entrepreneurial student who was accepted to UCLA. He started his Internet-based business in junior year and by senior year it consumed him. He simply could not let go. "His grades plummeted and he was more into making money." Eventually he closed the business but by that time his academics had suffered deeply. Meanwhile, UCLA checked his second-semester senior grades and rescinded his acceptance to the college. Yes, colleges can do that and so can scholarship providers.

Okay, enough doom and gloom. Ms. Kelsey also shared the story of some inspired students who used the Internet to travel to South America. The students she described were members of a youth fellowship in Santa Monica who created a MySpace page to garner support for their missionary trip to Peru. "They posted their goals, their pictures, and information about the needs in Peru," Ms. Kelsey said. "The site gained in popularity and people made online pledges." The effort was a success.

As you consider both student stories, think about how you can make technology work for you in your quest for scholarships.

Blogs

Anyone with a computer and an Internet connection can start a blog for free. A blog is a Web log or online journal where people write about a particular subject, document an occasion, or share random thoughts. I write a blog on my website. Students like you have started blogs for youth action groups, youth ministries, gaming, anime, sports, music, and more.

Imagine that you're all fired up about the curfew in effect in your town and you start a blog to share your thoughts. Who will read it and how far will your message go? What if readers add comments that include foul language or derogatory names? Will you be connected to these people forever in Internet history? How will you respond? How will your blog affect a scholarship sponsor's opinion of you? Positively or negatively? The good news about blogs is that, for the most part, you are in charge and you can craft your image.

For students who think that their screen names will protect them, think again. The amount of personal information you share can definitely connect you to like-minded people, but it can also be used against you. Will people use your information for good or evil?

Search Engines

Engine. It's the perfect word to describe the little tool that saves you a lot of time. You are probably very familiar with stand-alone search engines such as Google or Yahoo, but have you tried their advanced features? The beauty of search engines is not only their speed but their accuracy in finding scholarships, scholarship sponsors, and financial aid information. If you are willing to wade through virtual mountains of scholarship information, then using keyword searches is a good method to uncover scholarships not found in the national scholarship databases. Refer to appendix C to uncover the jargon used in the financial aid and scholarship world. Be prepared to do some speed reading to figure out if you match the criteria. Another quick way to find active scholarships is to add the word *winner* to your search. See my hot tip for another search-engine method.

HOT TIP

One of the more creative ways of digging up scholarships is to search images on the Internet. I have found this to work best on Google.

Instead of searching for scholarships in a major search engine and receiving a list of websites, go to the image-search function and add your criteria. For example, type in *scholarship* and the name of your state and select "images." You can narrow it down by adding *winner* to the search terms. Try substituting your city name for the state name to get a different list of results, or add the city name. You will see pictures of smiling scholarship winners and sample application forms. The image itself is usually linked to the source website. How convenient. Even if the picture is a few years old, you can find the sponsoring organization's name or website. This method casts a wide net and is not tailored to your specific profile. It allows you to see who else is winning what types of scholarships in your locale and it supplements your search for websites.

101

Scholarship Databases

Websites abound promising to connect you with millions of dollars in scholarships. "Sign up here! Free search! Join now!" they beckon you. In chapter 7, I shared some basics about finding scholarships on the Internet, but let's take a closer look at these databases.

The students I interviewed for this book used fastweb.com or scholarships.com in their search for scholarships. These are my two favorite online providers of scholarship information, and they each offer their own substance and style of scholarship searching. Their online search engines are easy to use and they quickly crunch the information you share to produce a list of matching scholarships. I have also used ScholarshipExperts.com but for some reason, I keep going back to my favorites. I recommend conducting your search using two or three sites to determine which ones provide you with the best matches for your profile. You want quality over quantity, so don't be swayed by the sheer number of matches.

How will you know which ones are quality leads? Ask yourself two questions: Are the majority of scholarships that come back in your matching list actually national contests or sweepstakes that require me to join another website? Are the dollar amounts and the effort required to win those awards quite small (such as "Enter to win $250! Submit a paragraph on how to save the world.")? I've got nothing against winning 250 bucks or saving the world, but my guess is that tens of thousands of other students are going to enter these easy, generic contests. The sites could be using their "scholarship opportunities" to gather the e-mail addresses of people like you to send you spam. Legitimate essay contests exist, and you may choose to enter them, but first determine if you are truly a good match and consider your competition.

Another question to ask is, Does the scholarship listing include the sponsor's name and website, and, if so, does it appear to be a reputable organization that is devoted to students or a "storefront" operation that is collecting your information for some other purpose?

You might think, "So what if they collect my information?" Look at it this way: If you were at a dance, a rodeo, a club, or wherever else you hang out and someone approached you and said, "Can I have your name, phone number, date of birth, high school, and e-mail address? If you give it to me, I *might* give you $250." What would you say? Think carefully about your value as a consumer on the World Wide Web. You, as a college-bound student, are a hot commodity.

The reputable scholarship search sites will tell you exactly how they plan to use your information (matching you with scholarships!), how they share your information (with marketing partners), and the nature of their privacy policies (opt in, opt out, confidential, etc.). Before clicking madly through the site, make sure you are comfortable with the policies. For instance, I don't mind sharing my personal information if the benefit outweighs the cost. Sure, it's free to sign up, but how long does it take me to use the service, how good is the information I'm going to get, and are the "offers" it sends me connected to my needs? *If the value of what I'm receiving exceeds my "cost" of participating, I'm fine with that.*

To be clear, the large national websites are able to offer their services for free because they have arrangements with marketing partners who are trying to reach students. In other words, it's free for you and the millions of other students who use it because someone else is paying for the chance to advertise products or services to you. You can choose to opt out of these advertising messages and offers when you sign up for the scholarship database and again, possibly, by changing the account preferences in your profile.

Before you complete an online profile on a scholarship-search tool, take out your scholarship worksheet and keep it next to you. Submitting an accurate profile will yield the best results for you. You want the information to be consistent among all of the scholarship-search tools you use.

Electronic Applications

The most technologically advanced scholarship programs are set up to communicate with you online and manage the entire application process electronically. Faster than you can text message your best friend, you can download an application from a sponsor's website. Some sponsors even *require* you to submit all of your information online. They may have sophisticated algorithms that help them categorize and score the applicants—all electronically. An automated scoring system generates a report on who qualifies, who doesn't, and who the top contenders are.

Other sponsors allow you to complete your application online, as a convenience to you, but they are printing out the responses and manually reviewing them. Depending on the length and level of detail, the application could take you five minutes or five hours (if an essay is required).

Many more scholarship providers use paper applications. They don't do this to torture you. They do it because that's how their business operations are set up. Also remember that these are charitable organizations and they may not have extra resources to transform their applications into paperless processes. Most sponsors still require you to fill out a form, type or word process your answers, and mail the application materials to the sponsor. This sounds old-school and can seem like culture shock to students who are plugged into new technology at a breakneck speed. The reality is, if you want to win scholarships, you will submit some paper applications.

If you are lucky enough to own a handheld device such as an iPhone or personal digital assistant (PDA), you can streamline your phone, e-mail, and Web access and certainly keep yourself organized, but I doubt you'll want to use it for scholarship searching.

If you're living off the grid or don't have technology resources at home, you can still be successful in your quest for scholarships. Follow the advice in *Scholarships 101*, but use free Internet access at your school or library.

No matter what level of comfort you have with technology, think about how it can help, or hinder, your success.

Fridge Notes

Think about your presence on the Internet. What might scholarship providers learn about you?

❑ How can you maximize free resources, use technology, and maintain a level of privacy that is comfortable to you?

_____

_____

_____

_____

❑ What creative ways can you use technology to assist and enhance your quest for scholarships?

_____

_____

_____

_____

❑ Who on your Team of Champions can assist you with technology if you need help?

_____

_____

❑ Which e-mail address will you use on your applications?

_____

❑ Which phone number will you use on your applications?

_____

❑ Where are you saving your scholarship worksheet, résumé, letters of recommendation, and applications? On your hard drive? On a jump drive? Did you create backups or multiple copies?

Chapter 11

_____

_____

The Buck Stops Here . . . and Here . . . and Here

W hat do you think it will feel like to win a scholar-ship? What will be expected of you as a newly awarded scholarship recipient? To answer these questions, let's imagine that you won your first scholarship!

Scholarship Award Announcement

> *As you grab the pile of mail on the kitchen counter, you notice an envelope addressed to you from the local community foun-dation. Your throat tightens up as you rip the top edge of the envelope in anticipation. As you begin to read the letter, your eye skips down to the bold print: **"We are pleased to announce that you have been selected as a scholarship recipient . . ."***

All of your hard work has paid off! Take a moment and think about what this means for you and your family. Can you feel the financial burden lifting from your shoulders? Your wallet?

Let the Celebration Begin!

Picture yourself holding a five-foot cardboard check with your name on it. You grin wide, the cameras flash, and everyone wants to shake your hand. This is a tangible, glorious moment on your path to college.

If you win one scholarship toward the cost of college, then you are a success! If you win $500, that's $500 more than when you started. When I've advised students and families, I'm struck by how many of them forget to bask in their success. Part of the problem is that no one is shoving fistfuls of money into your pockets. The money is real; you just can't see it. Ten thousand new one-dollar bills would weigh about twenty pounds. Would that fit in your backpack?

Imagine, if you can, what it feels like to *not* take out a student loan or to *not* make a student-loan payment six years from now.

So whether you earn $500 or $50,000 in scholarships—please celebrate! Here are some inexpensive and meaningful ways to acknowledge your success:

- Give yourself a day off—no chores, no homework, no practice.
- Text, call, or e-mail everyone you know to share your good news.
- Invite your Team of Champions to your house to celebrate.
- Take a picture of yourself for your scrapbook.
- Send an announcement to your local newspaper.
- Go out to dinner/pizza/ice cream with your family or friends.
- Write a special note to the person you addressed in your dream letter.

If you are chosen as a scholarship recipient, the first notification you will receive is likely to be a letter. (It could be a phone call or an e-mail, too). The scholarship provider may also notify your school. Although it is hard to focus on the details, you have a few more steps to complete before that cash makes it to your college. There is a common chain of events after you receive your scholarship award letter.

Verification and Terms

Attached to your scholarship letter may be a verification letter or form (see figure 11-1 for help understanding what the letter says). The purpose of this letter is to provide the sponsor with current information that will validate your selection as the winner and provide information about your intended college choice. *The sponsor wants to make sure that what you said on the application is still true.*

For example, if you won the scholarship based on academic achievement, the sponsor may request a copy of your most recent report card or your final transcript from high school to check your academic standing. If the scholarship requires you to attend college in your state but you have now made plans to attend an out-of-state college, you may no longer qualify for the scholarship. Basically, you need to disclose your situation honestly. Deadlines are just as important now as when you first applied.

The sponsor may also include a "terms and conditions" document that outlines how it will do business with you and your college, how and when

Terms Used	What They Mean
Applicant, candidate, recipient, nominee	YOU, the student
Sponsor, donor, provider	THEM, the people giving the scholarship
Ceremony, luncheon, banquet, reception	A CELEBRATION in which you may or may not have a significant role
Post-secondary institution	College, university, technical, or trade school
Financial aid office	College department that manages all forms of financial assistance including grants, loans, work-study, and scholarships
Bursar's office, cashier's office, or business office	College's financial hub, responsible for issuing tuition bills and collecting payments
"Good standing"	A favorable status, as defined by the provider, that you must maintain in order to receive your scholarships
"Enrollment verification"	Proof to the sponsor that you are actually attending college; often required in order to receive the disbursement

Figure 11-1. Deciphering the award language.

it will send payments, what is expected from you, and how to maintain the scholarship if it's a multiyear commitment.

Thank You

When you send back your verification form, this is the time to thank the sponsor. You can print a typed formal letter or send a handwritten note. Be sure to sign it with your full name, legibly written, because the sponsor may have several scholarship students that year. You might want to reiterate a point from your essay, because sponsors will often share the thank-you letters with staff, donors, and board members. They are not likely to share your original application, because it may be deemed confidential information.

I know from working with scholarship sponsors that not every scholarship winner sends a thank-you note. This is troubling and puzzling to me. If someone walked up to you on the street and gave you $5,000, wouldn't you thank the person?

You should also thank your Team of Champions. Simple, handwritten notes are fine, and they only take a few minutes to write. Maybe your helpers prefer hugs. That works, too. As a busy, college-bound student this might not seem like a high priority but it is. Gratitude is a key attribute of successful scholarship winners.

Recognition

Are you ready to be a celebrity? Long before you filled out a scholarship application, someone donated his or her hard-earned cash to help send you to college. The person only knows you on paper and possibly from a short interview, and the person might want to see you. Awarding money to you is probably a big deal to the sponsor and the sponsor's family members, staff, employees, volunteers, or other members of that organization. If you are invited to a scholarship banquet or awards ceremony, I advise you to go. Remember to pack your bag of scholarship-winning traits: confidence, enthusiasm, humility, and gratitude.

Your invitation may say, "You and a guest are invited," "You and a family member are invited," "You and your mentor are invited," etc. Sponsors usually extend the invitation to you and at least one other person so that you will feel comfortable and that person can share in the experience. Think about whom you would like to bring.

You might be thinking, "What happens at these events?" I'll admit I'm a sucker for scholarship ceremonies. Short ones, at least. This is where people like me meet people like you. Here's a synopsis of scholarship-award ceremony tips and what to expect.

■ **Accept the invitation if you can.** The entire event may be devoted to the scholarship winners, or you simply may be asked to stand and people will clap for you. Look good, smile, wave. Bask in their applause.

■ **Mingle, introduce yourself, converse.** You and other winners may wear name tags identifying you as special guests. You may be seated at a head table or near the podium. You may sit with the scholarship judges, the actual sponsors, or your fellow students.

■ **Act like you belong there.** If it's a pep rally at your school, don't sweat it, but if the event is at a four-star hotel, try to look nice. Okay, I don't want to sound like your mom, but you get the point. Go back to the interviewing skills you learned and use them here.

■ **Enjoy your fifteen minutes of fame . . . or one minute.** The event planners might ask you to give a short speech on winning the scholarship, read your essay, accept a certificate or award, shake hands with a dignitary, or pose with one of those big prop checks. They might snap your photo, too. Personally, I am disappointed when students are *not* given the opportunity to respond in some way. If they offer you a chance to say a few words, be brief and be thankful, but let your personality show.

■ **Stick around.** Try to keep your schedule open immediately after the event. The planners may want to take your picture with your family, take a group picture of the scholarship winners, or just chat with you about your plans for college. It's the least you can do if they just cut you a big, fat check. When I go to scholarship banquets I always want to meet the students' families to congratulate them, and this usually happens before or after the event.

"Hey, Scholarship Lady, what if I don't want to go because my family's going to embarrass me?" you ask. I feel your pain. At a homecoming game where I was being recognized, my younger stepbrother started picking his nose on the field during the halftime ceremony. Ugh. My advice, although it seems impossible, is to go regardless of what unknown embarrassments may occur. You'll at least have a good story to tell when you're old.

Your High School

As you begin to win scholarships, take time to alert your guidance counselor or designated scholarship coordinator. It makes school leaders feel proud when their students win scholarships. They will probably submit a scholarship report to the principal's office or school district to document who won which scholarships. Your school may ask you to complete a standard form that asks for the scholarship name and dollar amount. This information might also go into a graduation bulletin or newsletter.

Update your scholarship worksheet and résumé to reflect all scholarship awards. Money follows money, and you want judges to see that someone else has already invested in you.

HOT TIP

Clucking All the Way to the Bank

At one of my workshops I met a young woman who said that her friends teased her relentlessly when the school announced that she won a scholarship from a fast-food chicken restaurant. They called her "chicken girl." Sometimes, that's the price you pay for winning scholarships. I think it's worth it.

Check out local and chain restaurants in your town to see if they offer scholarships. The scholarships might be available to the public or current and former employees. If you win, can you handle the new name of "burger boy" or "pizza girl"? Sounds appetizing to me.

101

Your College

Sponsors try to follow the academic year, and most of them like to wrap things up by the end of the school year. You can expect notification of your awards by May or June at the latest, in anticipation of fall enrollment. It is your duty, as a scholarship recipient, to inform your college of all scholarships that you won. I advise you to do this in writing and spell out very clearly the terms of those awards. It might be easier to make a phone call or send a quick e-mail, but you want documentation of what you sent. The college may provide you with a simple form to document "all outside sources of funding." This is where you list your scholarships.

You are required, by law, to notify the college of your scholarships because, *according to the U.S. Department of Education, your financial aid cannot exceed the cost of attendance.* I know of scholarship students who have come close to tears because they did not understand this rule and were shocked when some of their nonscholarship financial aid was held back. "But wait," you ask, "Isn't that MY money?" No. Technically, financial aid is someone else's money that schools either grant, loan, or award to you. I urge you to read the sidebar on Scholarship Superstars to better understand the cash flow of scholarships.

If you applied for financial aid, and I'm assuming you did, then your college sent you a financial aid award letter. It lists explicitly the "package" assembled by the college to help you pay for the cost of attending. It may include a mix of grants, loans, institutional aid, work-study, and scholarships, or it could be all loans. It depends on your family's income profile, the cost of attending that college, the level of financial resources at that college, your eligibility for grants, and your scholarships.

Once you inform the school of your new scholarships, it must adjust the other forms of financial aid to remain compliant with federal law. It cannot "overaward" money to you (there is an exception made for Pell Grant recipients under certain circumstances). Schools must maintain, in writing, their disbursement and displacement policies. These policies can change each year, based on how much money the college has in its coffers, the availability of new government grants, and a variety of other internal and external factors. These policies describe how student aid is awarded, when payments are made against your student account (usually once per semester), and when you can expect to receive a check (usually during the first few weeks of the semester).

Quick Terms

Disbursement: The payment or transfer of money.

Displacement: Replacing one financial aid resource with another.

HOT TIP

Students and parents: Financial aid checks may not be available until the first or second week of classes. Unfortunately, you will need money to buy books right away. Plan for this cash crunch, and you will save everyone a lot of stress.

The best displacement policy, from a student's point of view, is one in which scholarships offset student loans first, then institutional aid and grants. Displacement of funds can be very confusing to a student, but remember: If you accumulate scholarship money above the cost of attendance, then you will not need the same financial aid package that the school originally presented to you.

If your temples are pounding after reading this section, imagine being a financial aid administrator who must calculate and recalculate financial aid packages for thousands of students.

Scholarship Superstars

You dreamed, planned, acted, and excelled your way to scholarship superstardom. Congratulations! Now the college has notified you that it is reducing your student-loan check or removing "institutional aid." What does this mean and why is it happening?

To refresh your memory, the federal government considers it your family's responsibility to pay for college, if you choose to attend. The cost of attendance (COA) less your estimated family contribution (EFC), is your financial need, according to the government. Here's the most basic way of looking at it: COA—EFC = Need.

The cost of attendance is different at each college. To make the math easy to understand, let's look at these figures:

College A		College B	
Tuition	$7,000	Tuition	$20,000
Room and Board	$8,000	Room and Board	$8,000
Books	$900	Books	$900
Travel	$600	Travel	$800
Misc. Personal Expenses	$1,900	Misc. Personal Expenses	$1,900
Total COA	$18,400	Total COA	$31,600
Your EFC	$6,000	Your EFC	$6,000
Need	$12,400	Need	$25,600

Here is an oversimplified illustration so that you can understand how winning outside scholarships affects your financial aid package. By "outside scholarships" I am referring to scholarships derived from private sources, independent of the college. These are most, if not all, of the scholarships for which you applied and won. The good news is that you were very successful at winning scholarships!

College A

Look at the figures for College A. In this scenario, the school packaged $12,400 for you in financial aid—the maximum allowable for need-based aid in this scenario. Let's say it included one state grant of $1,000, institutional aid of $5,000, and student loans of $6,400. Great. Over the summer, you notify the financial aid office that you won $4,000 in outside scholarships. College A follows its policies and applies that $4,000 against the $12,400 of other financial aid. It reduces your student loan from $6,400 to $2,400. The state grant and the institutional aid that do not need to be paid back are still in your package. Your new loan amount is $2,400. Your family still has an EFC of $6,000. You decide to get a part-time job, shop at the dollar store for all of your necessities, and live on ramen noodles. Not healthy, but affordable, and livable.

What if you earned more in scholarships? Let's say you won $11,000 in outside scholarships to attend College A. Great. The financial aid administrators at College A will take the $11,000 and apply it toward your financial aid package of $12,400. They will eliminate your student loans of $6,400 and take back the $5,000 that they contributed from their pool of money called institutional aid. The $1,000 state grant is still included in your package. Your family still has an EFC of $6,000.

Hang in there. I have one more example that affects students who accumulate more than the cost of attendance. What if you earn $21,000 in outside scholarships for your first year of college? Congratulations! You are a lean, mean, scholarship machine. If you attend College A, you will exceed the cost of attendance by $2,600! By exceeding the cost of attendance, you will not receive any loans, institutional aid, or grants (with the exception of a Pell Grant, if you qualify) because all of your financial need is met—but then what happens to the extra $2,600?

First, please feel good that you were successful at winning so much scholarship money. Next, immediately read your scholarship documentation to see if the money must be spent in the year it was awarded or if it can be reallocated to another year. If it is not clear, call or e-mail your scholarship provider. Good thing you kept track of names, phone numbers, and e-mail addresses on your scholarship tracking tool, right? Whether your scholarship provider will allow you to roll the money over to the following year is entirely its decision. Remember, technically speaking, it's not your money yet. For financial reasons, it may not be able to allow a rollover and will award the scholarship to another student. This is rare.

If the sponsor approves the rollover and allows you to save it for your second year of college, alert your financial aid office. It will probably ask for documentation, which can be a simple letter from the scholarship provider. The university may be able to hold the money in your student account for next year's college costs. All is good.

College B

Let's briefly look at College B, using the same outside scholarship scenarios: $4,000, $11,000, and $21,000. At the $4,000 and the $11,000 level, your scholarships will "displace" the other aid, but your need is still not fully met. Even with $21,000 in outside scholarships, you still have a financial aid need of $4,600, according to the calculation. In addition, your family is still expected to contribute $6,000. It would take another $10,600 in scholarships for you to completely pay for the cost of attendance at College B in cash your first year.

The reason I share this excruciating detail is to illustrate the impact of your scholarship dollars. To keep yourself motivated, just remember that every dollar you win in scholarships is one fewer dollar that your family has to pay for college, either by being applied to your EFC or through a reduction in student loans.

CASH FROM CAMPUS

As I began the interview with Ms. Jennifer McKenzie-Flynn I sensed urgency in her message. Her position as director of advancement and public affairs in the College of Letters and Science at the University of Wisconsin-Milwaukee requires her to use freshman scholarships as a recruitment tool or for students who have declared their majors. She sincerely wants *Scholarships 101* readers to understand how these funds are different from private scholarships and how you can best position yourself for similar scholarships at any college.

"My number-one job is to help students," Ms. McKenzie-Flynn shared with me. She manages scholarships to meet the needs of the donors, the college, the university, and the students.

The differences in the scholarships she manages are noteworthy. Faculty and staff contribute funds for freshman scholarships and they play an active role in calling potential students and encouraging them to attend the college. The faculty and staff also participate as scholarship judges. Their main motivation is to convince you (if you are a high-achieving student) to attend their campus. Scholarships for upperclassmen are usually funded by private donors. "Most of these donors are interested in helping specific majors or someone just like them. It could be the same high school, same interests, a hard-working student, not necessarily the highest achieving," Ms. McKenzie-Flynn explained.

She doesn't receive large quantities of unsolicited applications for freshman scholarships, because she does very targeted outreach to students who meet the criteria and have demonstrated academic achievement. "We're trying to court the student," she said.

In addition to recruiting students, she is also a liaison between scholarship students and other departments on campus. For instance, if a freshman scholar needs help securing a dorm room or completing some paperwork, she's there to help the student navigate through the university. That's a nice bonus for a confused freshman!

Ms. McKenzie also acknowledged that focusing on diversity is important for campuses across the country but she added this: "Diversity has so many elements, not just the color of one's skin." She said diversity is broadly defined to include geography, religion, race, socioeconomic status, disability, and gender. In addition to achievement and diversity, the likelihood of success on campus is a determining factor. Some of the most common mistakes she sees with freshman scholarship candidates are:

- Students who change their minds about attending the college and don't alert her. Meanwhile, other students could use the scholarship money. *Tip: If you change your mind, alert the sponsor. Don't let other students suffer.*

- Students who neglect the instructions and qualifications. *Tip: If you don't qualify, don't apply. If you do, follow the directions!*

- Students who clearly did not write their own essays or wrote essays that aren't genuine. *Tip: Submit compelling original work that showcases your academic goals.*

Ms. McKenzie-Flynn is also deeply concerned about financial issues for college students. "As the cost of education goes up, it is becoming more out of reach for families," she said. Another issue is that some students are very successful at accumulating scholarships but "fritter away" the money, neglecting to pay their bills first. For some students it's the first time they've had their own money and "they don't know how to handle it," she said.

When you apply to colleges, realize that people like Ms. McKenzie-Flynn may be calling you, and if they do, call back! Scholarships for incoming freshmen are very competitive, but realize that if these folks call you, it means you're a hot commodity.

The Bursar

The financial aid office is where you go for assistance in finding money to pay for college. The bursar's office is where you go to actually pay the bill.

Every student is, in essence, a customer of the college. The college charges you tuition. You, with the money you've assembled from a variety of sources, are expected to the pay the bill. The timing of your scholarship checks can affect how much money is in your student account and how much has been applied to your bill. The first few weeks of college are marked by a flurry of financial activity as funds come in from multiple sources. Much of this is handled electronically between the bursar's office and the financial aid office.

It can be very confusing, stressful, and frustrating for a student to get a bill for thousands of dollars when he or she knows that the money is coming soon. Pay close attention to your student account balance, bills, and records of payment. If you do not see your scholarship amounts applied toward your balance, be sure to double-check with the financial aid office. Most sponsors want to know that you are enrolled before they send their checks, but your tuition may be due before that check arrives. Colleges know this and are prepared to expedite money quickly. If you've never been to college or seen a bill for $10,000, it can be very intimidating to make it through this financial maze. Be patient and be persistent. The portion of financial aid that is left after your bills are paid may be distributed to you in a check or through an electronic funds transfer into your personal bank account. Visit your college's website to learn specifically how it processes outside scholarship checks.

Check Endorsements

Sponsors can issue a check in one of three ways:

1. *Payable to the college that you will attend.* The sponsor might send it to you or directly to the college, which will result in faster processing. You are not required to sign the check.

2. *Payable to you and the college.* The sponsor might send it to you or directly to the college, but you must sign the check.

3. *Payable to you.* The sponsor will send the check to you. You sign it and deposit it in your personal bank account. You are legally required to report the scholarship to your college and to use it for the cost of college attendance.

Keeping the Money Flowing

If you won a multiyear scholarship, give yourself an extra pat on the back. These are among the most competitive scholarships, and you will be expected to maintain your achievement level to keep the award across the years. Your scholarship provider may rely on you to send a copy of your grades each semester or it may have asked you to sign an education-information release form that allows it to request information directly from your college. Either way, it will be checking to see if you remain in "good standing" at the college. If you want your sponsor to keep sending the checks, then you need to keep up the good work.

Some providers may also include a morality clause in the terms and conditions of their scholarships. This means that the sponsor may pull the remainder of the scholarship if you run naked through the quad on a triple-dog-dare . . . and your friends capture it on video . . . and upload it to the world's largest online social-networking site . . . and the scholarship provider sees it. Ugh. Can you see the scholarship dollars evaporating?

Quick Terms

Four-Year Scholarship: The sponsor makes a four-year commitment to you. Similar to a renewable scholarship, except that the sponsor tells you up front that it will support you as long as you remain in "good standing." In most cases, you do not have to reapply each year. Sometimes this scholarship is called a "continuing" scholarship.

Full-Ride Scholarship: A scholarship whereby the sponsor will pay tuition, room, and board, and in some cases, the entire cost of attendance. It is most likely renewable for four years or until you earn a degree. These are the most coveted, in financial terms, of all scholarships.

Half-Tuition or Full-Tuition Scholarships: The sponsor will pay half or all of the "list price" of the tuition at your college. It could be renewable for four years. These scholarships are rare, valuable, and among the most competitive.

One-Time Gift: The sponsor awards the money to the scholarship recipient once. Recipients cannot reapply, because they no longer meet the criteria (incoming freshman) or, as winners, they are prohibited from applying again. These are the most common private scholarships.

Renewable Scholarships: Scholarships awarded with the understanding that students may be eligible for another award if they reapply or maintain eligibility, as determined by the sponsor.

Negotiation 101

Colleges compete for the best and brightest students because they know that those students can be choosy about where they attend college. They use preferential packaging to offer those students more scholarships and grants in the financial aid package than they offer to less desirable students. If you are a very high-achieving student or have a highly sought-after talent, you can use that to your advantage and earn more scholarships without completing another application. Preferential packaging is a little controversial because it doesn't necessarily focus funds on the neediest students, but on the students whom the college wants most.

I recently worked with a student who was very high-achieving *and* financially needy. I coached her through a negotiation with a college because her parents were not able to help her. She asked for my help because she received very generous offers from two schools, but her first-choice school did not produce the best offer. Her first-choice school would have left her with $3,000 in unmet need toward tuition and room and board.

Some families can easily write a check for $3,000. Her family could not. *By making one phone call she was able to get her dream college to kick in $2,000 more.* She still had to come up with $1,000, but she was able to attend her top-choice college.

It takes great diplomacy and guts to negotiate with a college, and there are many preconditions for it to work. And to be very clear, I am *not* advocating that every student who doesn't like his or her financial aid package should call the prospective college and complain. No! Please don't do that. You will unnecessarily burden the financial aid administrators and I will receive hate mail from them.

I am advocating that if you are in a situation where colleges are competing for your attention, and your top-choice college is close to matching your needs, it's worth a phone call to see if it can enhance your financial aid package to help you make your decision. Some colleges will not accept your request over the phone—do not be discouraged! Take this information and send a letter instead.

Quick Terms

Preferential Packaging: The practice of using institutional aid (scholarships and grants) to lure or recruit students to a college. Less emphasis is put on self-help aid.

Self-Help Aid: The part of a financial aid package that is the student's responsibility, such as loans and work-study.

Let's imagine that College A is your top choice—your dream college—and College B is your second choice. They have both sent you an offer letter, or award letter, but the offer from your dream college isn't as generous as the other college's. You might want to alert College A of the situation. Here's my advice.

Preconditions

Your negotiation is more likely to work if four things are true:

1. You are an excellent, sought-after student who has received multiple acceptance letters and generous financial aid award letters. If this does not describe you, then you really don't have much negotiating power.

2. In the financial aid mix, the colleges are offering major institutional aid near the same level. It might be a $15,000 scholarship or full tuition. This shows that they really want you. It's also important that the offers be near the same level. For example, if College A offered you $3,000 in institutional aid and College B offered you $12,000, it is not likely that College A will match that, because it would mean quadrupling its offer.

3. You are willing to call College A, your dream college, using every ounce of diplomacy in your being.

4. The college has ample resources and the ability to modify the package. This is important for you to understand, because some schools operate on a rigid "first offer, best offer" policy and they cannot kick in more money just because you called. In other situations, much like the college where I worked for seven years, the college does not have huge discretionary funds, meaning that its pool of scholarship dollars is quite limited and you really are lucky to have its current offer. Unfortunately, you may not know this until after you call.

Want vs. Need

You sincerely want to attend College A, but it isn't offering you as much institutional aid as College B. This means that you would end up with more loans to attend College A. Before you call College A, determine what you want and need and what *College A* wants and needs. College A obviously wants you to attend. The school doesn't need to be hassled. It does need to know where it stands in your decision-making process. You will need to share details about College B's offer, and you may need to provide proof of that offer to College A.

Preparation

If you are a high-performing student, chances are you made it on someone's radar screen during the admissions process. You want to call the person with whom you've had the best relationship. If you met or talked with a recruiter, it is probably that person. If you are not sure, start with the director of admissions. People in this department work with prospective students. Admissions and financial aid work together in what is known as "enrollment management." Place both offers in front of you and practice what you will say.

Making the Call

Generally speaking, call during business hours and do not call close to the end of the business day. People are trying to wrap things up and you don't want to rush your conversation. Your contact at the college will most likely need time to consider the adjustment to your financial aid package and connect with the other decision-makers at the college. If you are successful and they offer you more in scholarships, thank them for their personal effort. Ask them when you will receive a revised award letter. If they say that they cannot change the financial aid package, still thank them for their time.

Negotiation 101: What Should You Say?

Before calling your dream college to negotiate, make sure that you meet all of the preconditions. Figure out the wants and needs. Prepare by practicing what you will say. Of course, the other person may respond, interject, or ask you questions during the actual call. Here are some key sentences:

- "Thank you so much for the generous financial aid package."
- "I was thrilled to see the amount of scholarships you included."
- "You are my top choice and I really want to attend in the fall, but *(Name of the other college)* just sent me my offer letter and it, too, is very generous."
- "You might recall that I plan to enter the *(fill in the blank)* program/department/major." (This is important because the aid could be tied to recruitment in a certain department or degree program.)
- "I really don't know what I'm going to do at this stage. I'd love to come to your campus, but the other college is offering me *full tuition/more scholarship money/fewer loans (whatever it includes)*."
- "Before I make my decision, I wanted to give you a chance to reconsider your package. Are you able to *(ask for what you want, such as an increase in scholarships)?*"

Remember, the school may or may not have the ability to adjust its package. If it operates on a "first offer, best offer" principle, then it won't budge. It's at least worth a phone call to find out!

As a scholarship winner, you do not need to become a financial aid expert. You do need to understand the process, though, so you can advocate for yourself and keep tabs on the money awarded to you. Remember, you are essentially a steward of someone else's money. You want to do a good job of spending it!

Fridge Notes

Scholarship Success Reminders

❑ **Respond.** When you win a scholarship, review the terms of the agreement and immediately return the signed materials to your sponsor.

❑ **Thank.** Definitely thank the sponsor, but thank your Team of Champions, too.

❑ **Celebrate!** Acknowledge your accomplishment. Attend the banquets and ceremonies if you can.

❑ **Revise.** Add the names of the scholarships that you won onto your scholarship résumé. This shows new potential sponsors that someone else thought you were pretty great.

❑ **Alert.** Inform your high school and college about the scholarship. Your high school will want to know so it can brag about you, and your college needs to know for financial aid purposes.

❑ **Continue.** Once you win a scholarship, your adrenalin should kick in, and that's the best time to apply for another one. Keep going.

Chapter 12

Scholarship
Service Projects

Consider this chapter an invitation to continue what you learned in *Scholarships 101* and spread the word. Students, parents, teachers, counselors, and precollege advisors should all read this chapter. You can download tools and share your experiences on the website at www.scholarship street.com.

I encourage you to continue your quest for scholarships based on the Dream, Plan, Act, and Excel methods. I also encourage you to share what you learn with other students at your high school. If you have already graduated, consider approaching your alma mater or another high school that needs your expertise.

I am going to propose three ideas for you to keep the *Scholarships 101* dream alive. If you choose to be the student leader of these initiatives, you will add a community service component to your résumé. You might ask volunteers from a local college to assist you. College students, just like high school students, take on community service projects on their own or through service-learning classes on their campuses.

These scholarship service ideas are presented in order of ease.

Scholarship Special Event

November is National Scholarship Month. Why not use that opportunity to invite local scholarship sponsors to a special event at your school? The purpose of the event could be to honor the sponsors or to invite them into your school to share their advice with the scholarship-seeking students at your school. Lots of schools have senior banquet night or scholarship banquet night, but those tend to celebrate the students. Yes, celebrating student achievements is important, but you could also celebrate the folks who dole out the cash so that students from your school can go to college.

Your first step is to find out if students, parents, or staff at your school would be interested in doing this. The benefit to your school is that students would hear firsthand from the scholarship judges and decision makers, and your school might garner some positive publicity.

Whom should you invite? You could invite scholarship coordinators from local colleges, people who volunteer as judges, or the scholarship sponsors.

Has anyone at your school ever calculated how much money one sponsor has contributed over ten years? Twenty years? That might be a good way to find out who the biggest contributors are. For example, at one school I worked with, all of the students wanted to apply for a scholarship sponsored by a local radio station. Each year there was a lot of buzz and excitement. The station gave out about $40,000 a year. That's a huge chunk of change. What no one realized is that many other sponsors gave out the same amount or more—they just didn't have a radio station to promote it. Knowing which scholarship providers already support students from your school is one way to build your invite list. Another method is to invite sponsors who aren't familiar with your school but should be!

Your celebration could be as simple as "meet the sponsors," with donuts and coffee; it could be an award at a pep rally; or you could host a panel discussion for students featuring the scholarship sponsors, judges, or coordinators. You could do all three. If you choose to do this, let me know how it goes.

Scholarship Clinic

Hosting a scholarship clinic for seniors in your school is a good way to boost the number of students who apply for scholarships and the quality of the applications. If your school already conducts scholarship clinics, you are lucky. Skip ahead. For those who are intrigued, let me explain how scholarship clinics can benefit you and your school.

Many schools will host a financial aid night where hundreds of families jam into the school cafeteria, library, media center, or the gym. School administrators or guest speakers deliver very general information about financial aid to a mass of people. It's not fun. In most cases, it's not personalized either. It's your parents and hundreds of other parents freaking out about paying for college. Generally speaking, these workshops do not offer detailed direction about applying for scholarships either.

In the weeks following those types of workshops, my former staff and I conducted scholarship clinics with high school seniors on an individual or small-group basis at schools during the day. Depending on the students' stage, I helped them find matching scholarships, complete their first applications, proofread their essays, or answer their burning questions. The students loved it because they could ask questions they were afraid to ask in a large group, and they got specific, personal advice. The counselors loved it, too, because they didn't have time for such in-depth sessions with every senior who needed scholarships.

Organization and Purpose

You can organize your own scholarship clinic at your school. The purpose of the clinic is not to teach students every aspect of scholarship applications in one class period, it is to help them with their most pressing needs. Often times there's just one thing holding someone back. One student might need to register with a national search site, another might need help cutting through the jargon on an application, and still another might just want someone to read his or her essay and offer feedback. Partnerships are important to keep this a no-cost event for your school.

I recommend that you find project partners to conduct the scholarship clinic, and most certainly you will need the support of your school administrators. The National Honor Society or another student group might agree to take on the scholarship clinic as a service project, but make sure that all scholarship-seeking seniors are allowed to attend, not just those with the highest grade point averages. A counselor, teacher, or student-activity advisor should agree to help you manage the project and make key decisions.

Logistics

So what does a scholarship clinic look like? Imagine a classroom or open area with stations set up for different purposes. Think of a buffet. Ideally you want a space that has a few computers, tables where people can meet and talk, and a semiprivate area for personal issues. The last point is important because part of applying for scholarships requires students to share personal information about their parents, their family income, their heritage, etc., and this makes people uncomfortable. You can make them more comfortable by offering a little privacy.

You will need five stations:

1. A sign-in sheet or registration area.

2. A separate table for personal discussions.

3. An application area where you will stock multiple copies of applications for the most popular scholarships in your area and a few of the national ones, too.

4. A table for working on applications, proofreading essays, etc.

5. A small bank of computers with Internet access and printers stocked with paper. Your library, computer lab, or guidance department might already be arranged to host a scholarship clinic. If so, that will save you some time.

Ideally, you should plan the clinic for a Tuesday, Wednesday, or Thursday in December, January, or February, before most applications are due. You could host the clinic October or November, but students tend to be immersed in college applications at that time. You should operate the clinic on the same schedule as your class periods. Students can attend during study hall, lunch hour, or as part of a college-prep class if they have one. It can be exhausting to run one of these clinics, so depending on the size of your senior class, you may choose to hold your clinic from first through fifth period, plus lunch, over two days. Much of this will depend on when your counselor, advisor, or administrator is available.

Scholarship Helpers

Who will be your scholarship experts at the clinic? There are two groups of people who can be the experts: people in your school and people in the community. In your school it might be an AP English teacher, a guidance counselor, or a student club advisor. Outside of your school, you could ask for volunteers such as precollege advisors, college scholarship coordinators, scholarship sponsors or judges, and current college students who've won scholarships. You will be able to recruit volunteers if the roles are clearly defined and you limit the time you ask of people. You will need at least two people to assist students, but schedule three people. One of the people should be from your school staff or be a very trusted community volunteer at your school, and the other person should be invited based on the expertise you need. Don't take just anybody—think first about who can do the job. Schedule the helpers in two- or three-hour increments, and if they volunteer for more, great!

The role of the helpers is to move students from where they are now to the next step. They need to understand the scholarship-application process, and they should have a good mastery of English so they can review essays or proofread applications. They should also like working with students. That seems obvious, but it's worth pointing out.

Remember, this is not a large group workshop, and you need to make sure that everyone gets personal attention. Try for a ratio of one helper for every six to eight students. You might start calculating the number of seniors who are going to college and start to worry that all of them will show up. It's just not the case. Not all seniors will show up. Not every student who is bound for college will apply for scholarships, and of those who do apply for scholarships, not everyone wants or needs help. Some students already have a Team of Champions who are helping them, and other students are too busy ditching class to come to the scholarship clinic. I'm just trying to be real.

What happens at a scholarship clinic? Students enter the room and sign in with a greeter. They are asked to look at the table of applications to see if they match any of those scholarships and are encouraged to take copies if they need them. The next available helper asks what kind of help the student needs. Sometimes the student doesn't know; the student only knows that he or she needs scholarships. If the helper doesn't know the student, the helper might also ask the student to describe his or her academic and extracurricular life. The helper is starting at square one with this student, so the helper shows the student the scholarship listing if your school has one, goes back to the table of applications to peruse those, and then asks the student to register with a national search site to get started. That's one example. Another student might not understand how to indicate financial need on a scholarship application—that conversation should happen quietly away from the other students.

If you agree to organize this event at your school, make sure you devote the time to do so. Again, I urge you to do this as a group project. For those who are skeptical that students can't help organize this kind of event, may I remind you of prom? If students can organize a dance for hundreds of students, including food, entertainment, decorations, ticket sales, chaperones, etc., they can certainly handle organizing a scholarship clinic with support from their counselors or teachers.

Scholarship Clinic Pointers

- Be prepared. Provide copies of popular scholarships. Make sure computers and printers are good to go. Prep your volunteers, if any, ahead of time.

- Choose helpers who are knowledgeable about scholarship applications, essay writing, or scholarship searches. Some people will possess all of those skills; others should be assigned a specific job such as proofreading.

- Promote the scholarship clinic with seniors and their senior-level teachers.

- Be clear to students about what they will gain: personalized help, application proofreading, scholarship-search assistance, answers to their questions, and whatever else is planned.

- Thank everyone who pitched in!

Scholarship Information Source

When I worked on creating an online, searchable scholarship database in Wisconsin, I had a team of paid researchers, programmers, and Web designers to help me, but you can produce your own scholarship information source quite easily if you keep it small and manageable. Look at your scholarship tracking tool. This could be the base for your efforts because you've already collected some scholarship information.

Your high school probably maintains a list of scholarships for which, historically, students from your school apply. This is common. You also learned from the students in *Scholarships 101* that although they registered with national search sites, they were very successful at winning local scholarships.

The idea of creating a scholarship information source as a community service project would benefit students at your school or all schools in the district, depending on the size of your project. Propose your idea to one of your teachers, advisors, or counselors to see if it's feasible at your school. Your project would need several components to make it work, and it might be a multiyear project. Remember that I said it could be done easily if you narrow the scope of your project. If you want a larger database, you will definitely need long-term help.

Groups such as National Honor Society, DECA, the school newspaper, the technology club, or others could handle the project with a dedicated advisor and students. You need people who can do research, collect information, design a database that interacts with your school website, market the new tool, and maintain the information year to year. Whether you are still in high school or headed to college, you could serve as the volunteer leader of the project. The first year would require a large commitment, but subsequent years would require only maintenance. At the most basic level, if your school does not have a list of local scholarships, simply creating the list would be beneficial and easily possible within one school year.

HOT TIP

Parents, mentors, and volunteers: If you are involved in a civic group that looks for service projects, why not offer your time and talent to partner with a local school to host a scholarship clinic or create a scholarship database? Perhaps some members of your group have experience in record-keeping, marketing, or technology. Look at your talent pool and decide how you can help local students. Take the ideas outlined here to start your project.

101

How do you start? Here are the basics.

Consensus and Goal Setting

You as the leader could present the idea to your counselor, principal, or student advisor, or you could take this on as a personal project if you are hypermotivated and have lots of spare time. I doubt that. I don't recommend doing this alone, because it could become a full-time job! Instead, build a Team of Champions for the project. Determine the need for this type of information at your school. Is there a desperate need or does your school already have a really good list that just needs an injection of new information or updates? In your own scholarship quest, did you uncover tons of local scholarships that no one at your school knew about? If you are heading to college soon, why not share the information you found and pass it along to the next senior class? Share this outline with those new seniors.

What are your goals? Determine how you will measure your success. Will it be a club project, a schoolwide project, or a citywide project? If you live in a small town, it's very possible you could create a scholarship database for the entire town.

Building consensus requires leadership skills. Your job is to let other people share in the ownership of your idea so that one person doesn't get stuck doing all the work. You know what I mean. After you build consensus, then you add structure. Within that structure, everyone has responsibilities. Tasks are assigned or volunteers make commitments to do their parts. The next sections describe what some of those tasks might be. The "you" that I address is the person responsible for that task, not necessarily you the reader.

Organization

How you organize the work and the workers is important to your success. Where will people work on this project? Determine the best headquarters. Will it be the guidance office, library, computer lab, or another space? Will students be allowed to work on the project during the school day or only after school, as a club activity?

Another part of organization is sharing information. When your research team determines that its job is done, other team members will need to enter the research team's information into the database. Once it is entered in the database, someone else should proofread the entries. After proofreading, determine whether the information is ready to be shared publicly, and if so, in what format. Will you keep paper copies in a common file cabinet? Who will have access to those files? Your answers to these questions will help you begin to form a timeline and process for the gathering and dissemination of the scholarship information.

Decide if you will present the scholarship information alphabetically, categorically, or by deadline. The way you organize it in your database and filing system may be different from how you organize it for your classmates or the end user. Strong organization and decision making at the beginning will allow your project to flourish and will save you precious time.

Gathering Resources and Commitments

As part of your consensus building, your school may consider applying for a small donation from a local business or from a community foundation in order to launch the project. Creating a new hub of scholarship information for your school might require these extra resources if you are starting from scratch. Another resource you might consider is to partner with a local service club such as the Lions Club or the Junior Woman's Club. It is part of their mission to help the community, and often they are looking for organizations with which they can partner for one year. This extra support will come in handy if you have a large project ahead of you. Also think about the people and resources in your building. Has one group agreed to work on the project, or will it be multiple groups? What is the level of commitment from the advisor?

Scope and Research

When I say scope, I'm not referring to minty mouthwash; I'm referring to the scope of your project and *how many* scholarships or *what type* of scholarships you will include in your database. The answer should flow from your goals. Before you begin, determine how much time everyone is willing to devote to the project. Determine what your resources are and what new resources you might need.

If you live in a small town, you could probably finish your research in one month. If you live in a large city, it could take more than a year. If you live in a huge metropolitan area, then go back and think about your scope. Maybe you should focus on the top fifty scholarships awarded to students in your school. Remember, you can probably find that in old graduation announcements or in the guidance office.

To begin your research, decide who will be responsible for scouring the resources we talked about: online, in print, word-of-mouth, and self-promotion. Use all of these, plus the resources at your school, to collect the information. What types of students are best suited to do research, make follow-up calls, or send e-mails to sponsors? Should you do the research in one semester and launch the program in the subsequent semester? That depends on how much work there is for you.

In this project, finding scholarships through promotion is important, but instead of the *self*-promotion that you learned about in chapter 6, you will promote your school and your project. You will alert local associations, membership groups, and the media so they know what you are doing. You will create a common form for collecting that information. In my experience, the same person who collects the information should enter that information into the database or list to reduce the chance of errors or misunderstandings. You should also create a one-page letter or nicely formatted e-mail that can be sent to people from whom you are requesting the information. The majority of the people may need a reminder, and it's also helpful to give them a form that they can complete on paper or as an attachment to your e-mail. Sophisticated scholarship search sites have an online entry form that sponsors can fill out at their convenience. For the scope of your project, you probably don't need that or the potential security issues. Keep it simple.

In subsequent years someone will need to verify the deadlines, dollar amounts, and record the changes in eligibility, if any. The adults in your school are bound to ask you, as they should, "Who will keep this information updated?" Think about that before they ask. That's why I suggest that one student group takes on the project and makes a multiyear commitment.

HOT TIP

Once you collect the basic scholarship information that first time, very little changes about the scholarships except the deadline!

101

Technology

Your decisions about technology depend on the long-term goals of the project and the commitment of talent and resources that people are willing to invest. Instead of relying on one volunteer who might design a killer multirelational database or create an online data-entry form that automatically populates your database, I advise you to take a team approach. You do not want the entire project stalled because your lead techie left for college. Nor does that person want to be pestered a year from now about how something works. Trust me. Instead, decide what tools you will use that can live beyond one person, one graduating class, or one club.

Spreadsheets and word-processing programs are common, and your school probably has those readily available. Every college-bound student should be able to use those tools. If you are advanced, maybe you know how to use a multirelational database. Although you probably know how to use a lot of technologies, you might not know how to *create tools* based on technology. If all of these terms are foreign to you, you are obviously not the person who should lead the technical side of the project. Find someone or an organization at your school that understands databases and websites. No worries, you have other skills!

For the person leading the technology, here are a few questions: How will information be stored and retrieved, possibly by multiple users? How will students enter scholarship information into the database? Who will create the database and protect the information from predatory applications (computer applications, not scholarship applications)? Will end users have search capabilities through a website, or is that too sophisticated based on the time you can devote and your level of knowledge? Will you keep PDF files of scholarship applications or simply provide links to the sponsor's website for more information? Will students who conduct research for scholarship information make it past the firewall? My guess is that you will need the technology coordinator at your school involved in some of these conversations.

Your school may be well equipped technologically, or it may be suffering with patched-up computers and sketchy Internet access, which is why I am asking you these questions. If all of this technology talk seems a bit much, then choose a low-tech alternative such as typing a list with all of the scholarship information on it. You could also simply enter the information into a spreadsheet and ask your school secretary or another administrator how to merge the data into another document so that each scholarship appears in a neat format on a long list. This is called a merged document. See the samples of fictional school scholarships in figure 12–1.

Presentation and Marketing

After all of that hard work, how will you present your project to your school or community? Sure, you could photocopy the list and put it in the guidance office or library, but why not team up with some students at your school who are good at marketing? These students could be part of a business club at your school. You might even decide to dedicate your project and all of its elements to the next senior class.

Go back to what you learned about marketing: product, price, promotion, and placement. Your promotion will only work if the other pieces are addressed.

In your case, think about the final form for your product. You could produce a new section on your school's website, a printed directory of local scholarships, a monthly bulletin of scholarships, or another clever idea. What is your final product, based on your goals?

Your price should be free because this is a community-service project. You also learned that people who charge students for scholarship listings are

Rising Star Scholarship
The Sophia Jackson Scholarship Fund
1234 W. Scholarship St.
Smalltown, MS 34567
555–555–1234

Deadline: March 1   Amount: $2,000
Criteria:
- Minimum GPA of 2.75
- Participation in one school stage play
- Acceptance to an accredited college that offers a performing-arts major

Requirements:
- Submit application with nomination signature
- A 500-word personal essay on what skills you gained from being in a play
- Semifinalists will be asked for an interview

Description: The Rising Star Scholarship is for students who particpated in high school theatre and plan to pursue a career in the performing arts. Leadership skills are important.
To Apply: Stop in the guidance office.

Lucille Chartrand Memorial Scholarship
Chartrand Family Foundation
4321 E. 56th Ave.
Brookside, MS 34568
555–555–3456

Deadline: April 1   Amount: $500
Criteria:
- Minimum GPA of 3.0
- Interest in journalism
- Must have worked on school newspaper, yearbook, blog, or other publishing-related entity

Requirements:
- Application with two letters of recommendation
- Samples of your work

Description: The Lucille Chartrand scholarship memorializes the first editor of our town newspaper. Preference for students from Brookside school district.
To Apply: Visit the website for more information: brooksidecourier.com

---

Future Engineers Scholarship
Southeast Engineers Association
5632 Treetop Lane
Smalltown, MS 34567
555–555–0987

Deadline: April 1   Amount: $1,000
Criteria:
- Minimum GPA of 3.25
- High-achieving student with interest in engineering
- Acceptance to a four-year college in the state with an intent to major in engineering

Requirements:
- Application with two letters of recommendation
- One-page essay on why you want to be an engineer

Description: None provided.
To Apply: Apply via e-mail with attachments to: future@southeastengr.com

Figure 12–1. Sample school scholarship list.

viewed as scam artists. Even though you are not a scam artist, it might jeopardize the integrity of your team if you tried charging people for what is essentially public information. Do not let people misunderstand the value of the product, though. It took your team serious time and creativity to organize the project, do the research, set up the technology, and produce the final product.

Be sure to acknowledge who "paid" for the new scholarship tool, through their time or donations, so that the users know they are getting this information for free because someone else made a sacrifice. Try the phrase "Made possible by a grant from (fill in the blank)," or "The directory is a project of the (fill in the blank) with support from (teacher names, volunteers, etc)." If you received any help from businesses or organizations outside of your school, then absolutely, positively make sure they are recognized for their contributions.

The promotion of your new scholarship tool is the most visible part of the project. Students might not see the actual scholarship database or the thick files of research you collected, but they will see the results. How will you promote your new scholarship listing, website, or database? You can use posters in the school, a press release to your local newspaper, an announcement sent home to parents, or a special event. Think about which students need the information most, and target them the best way you can. If you have a scholarship resource that benefits students beyond your school, then brainstorm ways to get the word out in the community.

Your last point to consider is placement. Again, this goes to your audience. Will your final product be available in print or on a website? If it will be on a website, then you need some sort of announcement telling people that. Placement is about where people can find and use your new scholarship resource.

Maintenance

After the excitement wears off, who will be in charge of doing the scholarship updates, distributing the information, and promoting the tool? I hope you determined the groups responsible for maintenance when you were starting the project. Their jobs will not be as intense as your job as the leader, but they will need to make a commitment. It would really be a shame to do all of that work and then have the project suffer a proverbial death upon your departure. Congratulate yourself and make plans to pass the baton to the next leader!

Event, Clinic, or Source?

After reading the three ideas, think about which one is most realistic at your school. Think about forming a team. If you are still wondering why I would propose that you do all of this extra work, then let me be more clear. As you begin to lead these projects, it will increase your understanding of scholarships. You will undoubtedly talk firsthand with scholarship sponsors, judges, and coordinators. Even if you can't apply for a particular scholarship, you will learn from the real experts: the people who have the money. Isn't that worth it?

Scholarship Service Project Dos and Don'ts

Do

- Share your idea with teachers, counselors, and principals to see if it's possible to do the project.
- Create a team to handle the project. Recruit school clubs and an advisor.
- Create a plan with clear goals and expectations. What will you do? By when? Who will do it? How will things be done?

_____

_____

_____

_____

- Practice a few keys of leadership: organization, delegation, diplomacy.
- Recruit volunteers for specific jobs, not just anybody.
- Thank the people who helped you.
- Keep applying for scholarships during the project.

Don't

- Start the project on your own.
- Try to handle the whole project yourself.
- Assume that everyone will pitch in equally.
- Forget to add the project to your scholarship résumé!

Chapter 13

College and Beyond

N ow that you've become an expert on how scholarships work, how to find them, how to apply, how to build a Team of Champions, and how to win, I want you to bring the scholarship worksheet, scholarship tracking tool, and this book with you to college. You can succeed in college if you follow the basic components of *Scholarships 101*, which are Dream, Plan, Act, and Excel, and incorporate some college-specific advice.

Let me share with you how your quest for scholarships will change once you are on campus.

First, you will be busy. When I hear back from students during freshman year they are equally exhilarated and exhausted. They are trying to fit as much life and living as they can into each twenty-four-hour day, and "looking for scholarships" doesn't make it to the top of their priority lists. Because you have already invested in yourself and your scholarship search, it's much easier to keep the engine going than restart it. Look at your schedule and devote at least one hour per week to continuing your search, and add extra hours for completing applications. If you don't schedule the time to do it, then it won't get done.

HOT TIP

Remember the combination 2–28–2000 as you size up your competition in college.

If you are surrounded in high school by successful peers who also won scholarships, you may have the misperception that winning scholarships is common. To the contrary, according to a study of private scholarships conducted for the National Scholarship Providers Association, about 7 percent of undergraduate students earn private scholarships averaging nearly $2,000 per student.

101

The next time you are in a class, imagine two of twenty-eight students waving two thousand bucks in the air. Make sure you imagine yourself as one of them.

Look around. Who is your competition? What kind of students do they appear to be? Do they have compelling stories to tell? Do they each have a Team of Champions assembled and ready to help, like you do? Are they financed by mom and dad? Some students who appear to be scholarship competitors are not because they don't need the money and they aren't applying for scholarships. As you review campus-based scholarships, ask the question, "How many people applied last year?" The answer is one quick measure of your competition.

You might also be tempted to reduce your efforts on scholarships because loans and credit cards permeate the college culture. You are urged to sign on the dotted line. It's much less work than a scholarship essay, right? Yes, but you have to pay back what you borrow *with interest*. I was able to survive freshman and sophomore year of college without any loans, but after that it was a necessity. This is not by accident but sometimes by design. Remember our discussion on preferential packaging? The colleges use their institutional aid to recruit freshmen, but in subsequent years they may replace that institutional aid with loans. This is perfectly legit as they try to manage their pool of money and the needs of all of the students. What it should do for you, however, is motivate you to continue your personal efforts in the quest for scholarships.

Here's the real deal that not many families understand about scholarships: sophomore year is rough. You no longer qualify for "incoming freshman" status and you haven't declared your major yet. You're stuck in the middle. No one is trying to lure you to a university and you haven't had a chance to make inroads in your desired department or major. My advice for you, as you approach second semester of freshman year, is to revisit your scholarship search heavily, in preparation for sophomore year. You might also spend time sophomore year investing in activities, interests, and volunteer work so that when you declare your major and become eligible for department-based scholarships, you are looked upon favorably. Planting the seeds of relationships is important, too. Join the student groups that interest you and connect with campus advisors. Follow the same advice you learned in high school, which is to surround yourself with the people who know about the resources.

Department Scholarships

The general scholarship listings on your college's website or in its financial aid guidebook might not capture all of the detail about individual college, department, or major scholarships. The sources of this information could be the deans, department heads, administrative staff, or student groups aligned in that particular field. Sometimes these scholarships are funded by annual receptions or scholarship banquets, successful alumni, local businesses, or by the staff of that department. What you need to understand is what motivates the sponsors. Department scholarships could be used to reward high-achieving students or ensure that needy students can continue their studies. Most are merit-based, though.

Department scholarships can be difficult to manage if the donor or original sponsor has set difficult-to-find or unrealistic student criteria. For instance, someone from your city may have graduated from an out-of-state college and created a scholarship for students from your city to attend that same college. These are the kinds of scholarships that are not necessarily well-known.

HOT TIP

Colleges use strict terminology to categorize their staff members, and it can be confusing for a student who is seeking resources. I wish I would have understood this better as a student because it was very intimidating to hear someone say, "Talk to your unit business rep," and have no clue what they were saying. You might also hear someone say, "Contact Doctor So and So." Huh? "I don't need a doctor," you might think. If no one else in your family went to college, you might not be aware that professors who have Ph.D.'s (doctorate degrees) are called doctors. Some like to be called professor, others insist on doctor. Just so you know.

In another titling quagmire, for example, my official *category* when I was employed at a university was "fixed-term, nonteaching academic staff," my official *title* was "Outreach Program Manager II" and my *working title* was "Director." My staff members just called me Kim.

If you are directed to speak to someone such as the scholarship administrator of your department, realize that the person may have a different title. His or her job category could encompass more than just scholarships. Be proactive and ask for a specific name and number of whom you should contact.

101

Invest in Yourself—Again!

What else can you do? You can continue using the scholarship worksheet and the scholarship tracking tool, but you will probably want to create a more traditional résumé. You campus career center can help you with that.

You can also work on creating your new, big, bad, college self! I think it's easier to build your profile in college because you have more control over your time, and as an adult, you are in charge of you.

In high school, much of your day was designed around rigid time structures and other people's wishes. In college, you build your own schedule. Make sure you schedule time for the experiences and opportunities that could lead to scholarships. Remember, it's not just about working a database to find scholarship leads, it's about talking to people and sometimes just being in the right place at the right time. Who will write your letters of recommendation for a college scholarship if professors or advisors don't know you? You may have been involved in every club and activity in high school, but what are you going to do in college? Basically, once you get to college, you are rebuilding your scholarship profile. When you go to internship, job, or scholarship interviews, the interviewers probably won't ask you what you did in high school. They want to ask, "What are you doing now?" Have a good answer.

Fridge Notes

Your college plan for scholarships:

❑ Dream, Plan, Act, and Excel—keep going!

❑ Reserve time to look for scholarships using the same methods: online, in print, word-of-mouth, and self-promotion.

❑ Invest in creating your new scholarship-worthy self.

❑ Meet the professors, deans, department heads, and secretaries—all of these people have access to scholarship information and resources in different ways.

❑ Join student chapters of professional associations and strive for leadership roles—these associations are often the repository of career-specific scholarship information.

❑ Community service and leadership are still important. Can you perhaps take one of the scholarship service projects and lead the effort at your old high school?

❑ Remember that finding scholarships for sophomore year can be rough. Don't give up.

Scholarship Success Boot Camp

A re you ready to work out your scholarship muscles? Shed those flabby excuses? Develop apps of steel? Scholarship Success Boot Camp requires a huge commitment and it's only for the most serious scholarship seekers. Not everyone will rise to the challenge.

So far you have known me as the happy-go-lucky Scholarship Lady who wrote this book to help students find money for college. Yep, that's me, but there's another side to The Scholarship Lady that will shake you out of your comfort zone; force you to put down the remote, the phone, or the controller; and tell you to wake up and smell the money. Opportunity is all around you.

Scholarship Success Boot Camp is for people who realize now that they might get a little lazy later. Boot Camp is a compact, intense version of *Scholarships 101*. You can join Boot Camp from the beginning or when you need a little push.

You Are in Charge

I know that some students need a little more direction than the rest. After reading the book, they'll write their dream letters. They'll ask one person to be on their Team of Champions. They will definitely register with a scholarship search site (because it's convenient and easy to do). They might even apply for one or two scholarships. If they don't win, they will feel dejected and disillusioned. They will tuck their essays away, stop using the scholarship tracking tool, and start applying for sweepstakes in hopes of striking it rich. They will start blaming other people. They'll move from feeling fabulous to feeling desperate. Don't let that happen to you! *Focus, my friend, focus!*

You know that most students who apply for scholarships don't win. That's the real world. You, however, have a whole set of tools to help you succeed. You have a Team of Champions. You have this book as your guide. You are in charge.

Realize that winning even one scholarship is a huge success. The students featured in this book won multiple scholarships, but I didn't know that when I chose to interview them. All I knew was that they had each won a single scholarship. What set them apart from their peers is that they never gave up. They kept applying for scholarships over the course of several months, and the feeling from winning one scholarship fueled their next efforts. Yes, they were good students; yes, they all had some form of community service or leadership traits; but so do thousands of other students. These students imposed strict discipline on themselves. No one could make them do it. They chose to keep going.

The Commitment

Are you willing to double-down on your efforts? Are you ready to take the extra step? Are you ready to rumble (with your own fears)? No excuses. No whining. Lots of hard work. In this basic training exercise I will distill the most important parts of *Scholarships 101*. I will ask you to dream bigger, plan better, act quickly, and excel beyond what you thought you could do.

Are you in?

Boot Camp Prerequisites

When you head to college you will learn that you cannot sign up for an advanced class until you've passed the prerequisite classes. I have prerequisites for Scholarship Success Boot Camp because I want you to be a success. You must complete three criteria before Boot Camp begins.

Criteria One—Eliminate the Fear Factor

This step pays tribute to Tanya, an admissions counselor in California who was a former co-worker of mine. Tanya was an average student in high school who thought that college was only for "smart people with money." She didn't think she would fit in. She didn't know anything about financial aid and no one else from her family had gone to college. So, she joined the Marines. After four years of military service and after serving in Desert Storm, she convinced herself that going to college couldn't be as scary as sitting in a foxhole in hostile territory. Tanya enrolled in college—and graduated magna cum laude! She has devoted her career to helping fearful students take the first step toward going to college.

If you have any doubts or fears about going to college, paying for college, preparing for college, fitting in at college, owing money for college, winning scholarships, or anything related to it, please talk to someone about it. Your fears and your hesitations could hold you back from scholarship success. You may unknowingly sabotage your own efforts. If people are filling your head with fear, ignore them and focus on your dream.

Criteria Two—Clear Your Calendar

Boot Camp happens now. The students who win scholarships are masters at balancing their time and investing in the process. Boot Camp requires you to abandon time suckers and make some sacrifices. Remember Minh? She worked on scholarships every Saturday for nearly six months. How about Karlton? He voluntarily enrolled in architecture programs during the summer. I won't tell you which day or which hours to pick, but you must make a commitment to stop doing something else so you can spend time in Scholarship Success Boot Camp right now. *Your original commitment will be six days*, preferably in sequence. Are you ready to do that?

Criteria Three—Come Hungry

I really do care about helping students win scholarships, but if those students don't care as much as or more than I do, then my advice doesn't make a difference. These are the students who write bland essays or miss deadlines. They don't appear "hungry," as one sponsor said.

When I ask scholarship judges, teachers, and youth counselors to tell me about trends they see, the one word that has surfaced over the years is *apathy*. Please don't send letters telling me that the majority of high school students are not apathetic—I know that! I have met hundreds of amazing students who inspire me. I feel safe and secure knowing our future is in their hands. Some students, however, don't really seem to care deeply about anything.

If you don't really care about your future or the future of the world around you, it will be difficult to convince a judge to care about you. To start Boot Camp, you need to be hungry for success. Are you hungry?

Boot Camp in Six Steps

You're fearless, you're ready, and you're hungry. You've met the prereqs for Boot Camp. Congratulations! Here we go.

Boot Camp Step One: Dream Bigger, Better, and Bolder

Go back to your dream. Does it inspire you, motivate you, or drive you to action? Is it outrageous, audacious, and bold? At the same time, is it concrete, with action steps on how you will accomplish your mission? If the boldest statement you can make is, "I want to go to college so I can make a lot of money and here's how I'm going to do it," I'm telling you now that you have some work to do. That dream might inspire Donald Trump, but it won't inspire the scholarship judges I know. You heard their advice: They want students who are hungry, students who care about themselves and their communities, students who have big plans, and students who are worthy investments.

Exercise One: Redraft Your Dream Letter

Your dream will help you build your Team of Champions, form the basis of your essays, and keep you focused. Cut the clichés. Give people something to believe in. Make it bigger, better, and bolder. Read it out loud.

Boot Camp Step Two: Invest in the Best

The key to winning scholarships is not to rely on a secret formula or hope for a lucky break. The key is in presenting your best self to the scholarship decision makers. Remember, scholarship judges will invest in you if it appears you have invested in yourself. Yes, you can win a scholarship with a 2.5 GPA, a little community service, and a good letter of recommendation, but you can win far more with a 3.0 GPA, a little more community service, and two good letters of recommendation. Boot Camp requires you to look hard at your accomplishments and make changes that will improve your Fabulous Factor.

You want a scholarship judge to stand up and shout out, "I want to help THIS student!" It could be your shockingly high ACT or SAT, or it could be your unbelievable commitment to community service. Is it your thought-provoking essay? Your strong desire to graduate from college and change the history of your family? You must stand out. Pick one thing you can invest in to improve your Fabulous Factor.

For example, this is *one* plan of how a student could boost his or her GPA in one marking period:

- Spend an extra thirty minutes a night studying the subject you enjoy the most.
- Spend an extra thirty minutes a night studying your worst subject.
- Participate in tutoring.
- Do extra credit every time it is offered.

Exercise Two: Increase Your Fabulous Factor

Choose one thing you can do to increase your GPA, increase your community service, improve your ACT or SAT scores, improve your recommendations, or give yourself an edge. Start today and stick with it until you see the result. Document that result on your scholarship résumé and update any other scholarship-related information. For example, update your GPA on your résumé, your scholarship-database profile, new applications, etc.

Boot Camp Step Three: Commit to a New Essay

Maybe you cranked out your first essay to meet a deadline and never went back. Go back now. If a scholarship application asks for an essay, then that means the essay is important. It might have a high or low weight in the award criteria, but a good essay is never going to harm your application. Every judge, sponsor, and student I interviewed acknowledged the need for better essays. This is not personal. It's not just you. This is about scholarship applicants in general. If you are not able to critique your own work, ask a teacher or someone on your Team of Champions to help you. Get more than one opinion. Think about structure, content, and style. Is your voice generic or personal? Does it make the reader yawn or flip the page with anticipation?

Maybe it's time to break up with your old essay. Few students keep their essays because they are prefect. They keep them because it's easier than starting over or editing.

Exercise Three: Recraft Your Essays

Write, rewrite, and write again. Write an essay that makes judges argue in your favor. Let them know who you are. If someone tells you your essay is "good" or "nice," you might be in trouble. Good, nice essays don't win scholarship competitions. Think about what you need. A better theme? More careful proofreading? A review of compositional techniques? Extra practice? If you are not equipped to help yourself, find help. The essay is too important to leave to chance.

Boot Camp Step Four: Nurture Your Team of Champions

Throughout the book, I discussed building your Team of Champions. These are the people who care about you most and the people who might not know you well but can help you. Give them a pep talk. Up until now, you've relied on them for help, which is important, but have a conversation with them that doesn't involve you asking for something. Listen to them.

Keep your Team of Champions up-to-date on your progress with a quick phone call, text message, or e-mail. If your team members live nearby, stop in to say hello. Remember that there are plenty of people who want to help you, but they don't want to feel used either.

Exercise Four: Support Your Team of Champions and Add Another Person

Inform your Team of Champions that you've entered a self-imposed scholarship boot camp. Let them know how you are doing.

Your team members need encouragement, too! It might be time to rotate your team members. Maybe grandma is tired of clipping newspapers or proofreading your papers. Who else can join your team? Look back at the scholarship road map and the bull's eye. Is there a person, place, or resource that you can bring in now that maybe you didn't think of before? Add one person to your team.

Boot Camp Step Five: Hunt Down Those Scholarships

When you search for scholarships in Boot Camp, the process is never complete. Here's an example: When I managed a local scholarship database, we launched our website with 250 scholarships in it. Yippee! The following year, we reached 500. In the third year we reached 700. People were astounded at what we uncovered. If you want to win scholarships, you need to look beyond the easy sources and dig deeper. Although I don't expect you to find 700 scholarships perfectly matched for you, I do expect you to increase the number of leads on your list.

Exercise Five: Increase Your Scholarship Leads by 50 Percent

Use the methods we discussed: online, in print, word-of-mouth, and self-promotion. Go back to the scholarship-search databases and try changing one thing about your profile. Revisit your favorite search engine and try different keywords. Look at newspapers in nearby cities. Check out the websites of other high schools or college-prep high schools in your city. Do they have scholarships that are new to you? Add them to your scholarship tracking tool and prioritize them. Follow up on your prospects and priorities.

Kelsey, a former Boot Camp participant, decided to use image searches to boost her number of leads.

High school senior Kelsey (right), and her mom Denise.

Boot Camp Step Six: Combine the Power of All of Your Tactics

The ultimate scholarship applicant follows these principles of *Scholarships 101*:

- Fund-Raising 101—Understand the difference between a lead, a prospect, and a priority.

- Assessment 101—What's the competition? When is the deadline? How much work is required? What are your true priorities?

- Marketing 101—Position yourself favorably using the basic marketing principles: product, price, promotion, and placement.

- Applications 101—Follow the class rules and increase the number of high-quality, compelling applications that you submit.

- Recommendations 101—Take extra time to draft the phrases that you would like to appear in your recommendation letters. Share these with new recommenders or request new letters from past recommenders.

■ Essays 101—Revise and rewrite. Recycling is banned from Boot Camp.

■ Persistence 101—Don't give up!

Exercise Six: Incorporate All of the 101 Techniques into Your Efforts!

Look at the 101 concepts and write down one way that you can immediately put each idea to work for you. For instance, for Assessment 101 you may choose to prioritize scholarships that receive fewer than fifty applicants each year. You make a pact with yourself that you will not submit any online scholarship contests or sweepstakes for the next thirty days. For Essays 101, you might agree to rewrite the introductory paragraph of your essay before submitting any more applications. Make these commitments to yourself in all 101 categories.

HOT TIP

The Boot Camp for Writers

My friend Debbie paid for and enrolled me in a boot camp for lazy writers. What a friend. I always intended to share my scholarship advice with students, but it took a kick in the pants to get me started. That's what friends are for, right? My drill sergeant, Judy, was a tough cookie with good advice and high expectations. We even had homework. This was on top of my regular job. Ugh.

101

What I gained most out of the boot camp was being around other writers. They were just as influential in my success as Judy and Debbie. They offered advice, words of encouragement, more than one reality check, and they cheered me on toward my goals. If you need help, gather some friends or other students who are in a scholarship struggle and ask them to join your boot camp. You can keep one another in check and you won't feel alone.

Fridge Notes

Boot Camp at a Glance

No fear. Make time. Come hungry.

Step One: Dream bigger, better, bolder.

Step Two: Invest in the best.

Step Three: Commit to a new essay.

Step Four: Nurture your Team of Champions.

Step Five: Hunt down those scholarships.

Step Six: Combine the power of your Dream, Plan, Act, and Excel commitment to these specific subjects: Fund-Raising 101, Assessment 101, Marketing 101, Applications 101, Recommendations 101, Essays 101, and Persistence 101.

Meet Me After Class, and Bring a Friend

Some of the best conversations occur outside of the classroom. That's how you know it was a good class: people keep talking about it. Likewise, *Scholarships 101* doesn't end here. You and your friends, parents, teachers, and Team of Champions are all invited to ScholarshipStreet.com, the place to be for scholarship seekers.

You can download all of the tools in this book, link to updated URLs for the websites I mentioned, read alerts on scholarship scams, and enroll in *Scholarships 101* classes. I don't want you to destroy the book, either, so all of the Fridge Notes will be available for you to print and put on your fridge or locker as reminders.

Share Your Story

The Scholarship Lady has one special favor to ask of you. When you win a scholarship, share your success story with everyone. I have a special section on my website devoted to you. Other students need to hear how you took the Dream, Plan, Act, and Excel process and made it work for your own situation. If you want to share your original dream letter, you can do that, too. If you have tips or advice for other students, they need to know. Send me your questions, and I'll add them to my Frequently Asked Questions section (with the answers, of course). I know that asking questions is part of learning something new, which is why I asked you so many questions in the book.

Don't Stress

I remember when it was time to potty train my daughter and I bought a neat little book and followed the advice, and everything went great until we both ended up crumpled on the bathroom floor in tears. We were so stressed out. I flipped through the book and the index, and I couldn't find anything on "your kid starts crying." Huh? A book on potty training that doesn't tell you what to do when your toddler is in tears is not a very helpful book. There was no website for reference. No helpful pointers. I felt abandoned.

That is the only book that I ever threw away in my life. I didn't want anyone else to suffer helplessly and needlessly. I won't let that happen to you. If you struggle with parts of *Scholarships 101*, I want to hear about it. I will post updates and extra advice on the website, based on what you need.

What Only You Can Do

Sure, I want to help millions of high school graduates go to college with cash in hand, but I'm only human. You know that I will *assist* you in your strategies to find scholarships, and I will *teach* you how to apply for scholarships, but the primary responsibility for managing your scholarship empire is up to you! In the real world, you will Dream, Plan, Act, and Excel your way to scholarships. You have my support and wishes for great success!

—The Scholarship Lady

Helpful Websites

All of the links below are subject to change. You can find the most current list of resources at www.scholarshipstreet.com.

Scholarships 101 Book, Blog, Boot Camp, Tools, and More!
www.scholarshipstreet.com

Testing Services
ACT
www.act.org

SAT
www.collegeboard.com

Precollege Program Lists
National College Access Network
www.collegeaccess.org

Pathways to College Network
www.pathwaystocollege.net

Financial Aid

FAFSA

www.fafsa.ed.gov

College Goal Sunday

www.collegegoalsundayusa.org

National Association of Student Financial Aid Administrators (NASFAA)

www.studentaid.org

Scholarship Searches

www.fastweb.com
www.scholarshipexperts.com
www.scholarships.com

Scholarship Scam Alerts

Federal Trade Commission

www.ftc.gov

State Higher-Education Agencies

Source: U.S. Department of Education, www.ed.gov.

These agencies administer state grants and sometimes scholarship programs. I highly recommend that you include a visit to their websites in your scholarship search. Although these agencies predominantly manage grant programs, they are also a hub of general postsecondary-education information. In some cases the state university system is the relevant agency.

Alabama

Alabama Commission on Higher Education
P.O. Box 302000
Montgomery, AL 36130-2000
Phone: (334) 242-1998
Toll-Free: (800) 960-7773
Toll-Free restrictions: AL residents only
Fax: (334) 242-0268
Website: http://www.ache.state.al.us/

Alaska
Alaska Commission on Postsecondary Education
P.O. Box 110505
Juneau, AK 99811-0505
Phone: (907) 465-2962
Toll-Free: (800) 441-2962
Fax: (907) 465-5316
TTY: (907) 465-3143
Website: http://alaskadvantage.state.ak.us/

Arizona
Arizona Commission for Postsecondary Education
2020 North Central Avenue, Suite 550
Phoenix, AZ 85004-4503
Phone: (602) 258-2435
Fax: (602) 258-2483
Website: http://www.azhighered.gov

Arkansas
Arkansas Department of Higher Education
114 East Capitol Avenue
Little Rock, AR 72201-3818
Phone: (501) 371-2000
Fax: (501) 371-2001
Website: http://www.arkansashighered.com/

California
California Student Aid Commission
P.O. Box 419027
Rancho Cordova, CA 95741-9027
Phone: (916) 526-7590
Toll-Free: (888) 224-7268
Fax: (916) 526-8002
Website: http://www.csac.ca.gov/

Colorado
Colorado Commission on Higher Education
1380 Lawrence Street, Suite 1200
Denver, CO 80204
Phone: (303) 866-2723
Fax: (303) 866-4266
Website: http://www.state.co.us/cche/

Connecticut
Connecticut Department of Higher Education
61 Woodland Street
Hartford, CT 06105-2326
Phone: (860) 947-1800
Toll-Free: (800) 842-0229
Fax: (860) 947-1310
Website: http://www.ctdhe.org/

Delaware
Delaware Higher Education Commission
Carvel State Office Building, Fifth Floor
820 North French Street
Wilmington, DE 19801
Phone: (302) 577-5240
Toll-Free: (800) 292-7935
Fax: (302) 577-6765
Website: http://www.doe.state.de.us/high-ed/

District of Columbia
State Education Office (District of Columbia)
441 Fourth Street, NW, Suite 350 North
Washington, D.C. 20001
Phone: (202) 727-6436
Toll-Free: (877) 485-6751
Fax: (202) 727-2834
TTY: (202) 727-1675
Website: http://seo.dc.gov/seo/site/default.asp

Florida
Office of Student Financial Assistance
Florida Department of Education
1940 N. Monroe St., Suite 70
Tallahassee, FL 32303-4759
Toll-Free: (888) 827-2004
Fax: (850) 487-6244
Website: http://www.floridastudentfinancialaid.org/

Georgia
Georgia Student Finance Commission
2082 East Exchange Place
Tucker, GA 30084
Phone: (770) 724-9000
Toll-Free: (800) 505-4732
Fax: (770) 724-9089
Website: http://www.gsfc.org/

Hawaii
Hawaii State Postsecondary Education Commission
2444 Dole Street, Room 209
Honolulu, HI 96822-2302
Phone: (808) 956-6624
Fax: (808) 956-0798

Idaho
Idaho State Board of Education
P.O. Box 83720
650 West State Street
Boise, ID 83720-0037
Phone: (208) 334-2270
Fax: (208) 334-2632
Website: http://www.boardofed.idaho.gov/

Illinois
Illinois Student Assistance Commission
1755 Lake Cook Road
Deerfield, IL 60015-5209

Phone: (847) 948-8500
Toll-Free: (800) 899-4722
Fax: (847) 831-8549
TTY: (847) 831-8326
Website: http://www.collegezone.com/

Indiana

State Student Assistance Commission of Indiana
150 West Market Street, Suite 500
Indianapolis, IN 46204-2811
Phone: (317) 232-2350
Toll-Free: (888) 528-4719
Fax: (317) 232-3260
Website: http://www.ssaci.in.gov/

Iowa

Iowa College Student Aid Commission
200 10th Street, Fourth Floor
Des Moines, IA 50309
Phone: (515) 725-3400
Toll-Free: (800) 383-4222
Fax: (515) 725-3401
Website: http://www.iowacollegeaid.gov/

Kansas

Kansas Board of Regents
Curtis State Office Building
1000 SW Jackson Street, Suite 520
Topeka, KS 66612-1368
Phone: (785) 296-3421
Fax: (785) 296-0983
Website: http://www.kansasregents.org/

Kentucky

Kentucky Higher Education Assistance Authority
P.O. Box 798
Frankfort, KY 40602-0798
Phone: (502) 696-7200

Toll-Free: (800) 928-8926
Fax: (502) 696-7496
TTY: (800) 855-2880
Website: http://www.kheaa.com/

Louisiana
Louisiana Office of Student Financial Assistance
1885 Wooddale Blvd.
Baton Rouge, LA 70806
Phone: (225) 922-1012
Toll-Free: (800) 259-5626, ext. 1012
Fax: (225) 922-0790
Website: http://www.osfa.state.la.us/

Maine
Finance Authority of Maine
5 Community Drive
P.O. Box 949
Augusta, ME 04332-0949
Phone: (207) 623-3263
Toll-Free: (800) 228-3734
Fax: (207) 623-0095
TTY: (207) 626-2717
Website: http://www.famemaine.com/

Maryland
Maryland Higher Education Commission
839 Bestgate Road, Suite 400
Annapolis, MD 21401-3013
Phone: (410) 260-4500
Toll-Free: (800) 974-0203
Toll-Free restrictions: MD residents only
Fax: (410) 260-3200
TTY: (800) 735-2258
Website: http://www.mhec.state.md.us/

Massachusetts
Massachusetts Board of Higher Education
One Ashburton Place, Room 1401
Boston, MA 02108-1696
Phone: (617) 994-6950
Fax: (617) 727-6397
Website: http://www.mass.edu/

Michigan
Michigan Student Financial Services Bureau
P.O. Box 30047
Lansing, MI 48909-7547
Toll-Free: (800) 642-5626 x37054
Fax: (517) 241-0155
Website: http://www.michigan.gov/studentaid

Minnesota
Minnesota Office of Higher Education
1450 Energy Park Drive, Suite 350
St. Paul, MN 55108-5227
Phone: (651) 642-0567
Toll-Free: (800) 657-3866
Fax: (651) 642-0675
TTY: (800) 627-3529
Website: http://www.ohe.state.mn.us/

Mississippi
Mississippi Institutions of Higher Learning
3825 Ridgewood Road
Jackson, MS 39211-6453
Phone: (601) 432-6647
Toll-Free: (800) 327-2980
Toll-Free restrictions: MS residents only
Fax: (601) 432-6972
Website: http://www.ihl.state.ms.us/

Missouri
Missouri Department of Higher Education
3515 Amazonas Drive
Jefferson City, MO 65109
Phone: (573) 751-2361
Toll-Free: (800) 473-6757
Fax: (573) 751-6635
TTY: (800) 735-2966
Website: http://www.dhe.mo.gov/

Montana
Montana University System
46 North Last Chance Gulch
P.O. Box 203201
Helena, MT 59620-3201
Phone: (406) 444-6570
Fax: (406) 444-1469
Website: http://www.mus.edu/

Nebraska
Nebraska Coordinating Commission for Postsecondary Education
140 North Eighth Street, Suite 300
P.O. Box 95005
Lincoln, NE 68509-5005
Phone: (402) 471-2847
Fax: (402) 471-2886
Website: http://www.ccpe.state.ne.us

Nevada
Nevada System of Higher Education
Nevada Millennium Scholarship Office
Office of the State Treasurer
Grant Sawyer Building
555 East Washington Ave., Suite 4600
Las Vegas, Nevada 89101
Phone: (702) 486-3383

Toll Free: (888) 477-2667
Fax: (702) 486-3246
http://nevadatreasurer.gov

New Hampshire
New Hampshire Postsecondary Education Commission
3 Barrell Court, Suite 300
Concord, NH 03301-8543
Phone: (603) 271-2555
Fax: (603) 271-2696
TTY: (800) 735-2964
Website: http://www.state.nh.us/postsecondary/

New Jersey
Commission on Higher Education (New Jersey)
20 West State Street, 7th Floor
Trenton, NJ 08608-1206
Phone: (609) 292-4310
Toll-Free: (800) 792-8670
Fax: (609) 292-7225
Website: http://www.state.nj.us/highereducation

Higher Education Student Assistance Authority (New Jersey)
4 Quakerbridge Plaza
Trenton, NJ 08619
Phone: (609) 588-3226
Toll-Free: (800) 792-8670
Fax: (609) 588-7389
TTY: (609) 588-2526
Website: http://www.hesaa.org/

New Mexico
New Mexico Higher Education Department
1068 Cerrillos Road
Santa Fe, NM 87505-1650
Phone: (505) 476-6500
Toll-Free: (800) 279-9777

Fax: (505) 476-6511
TTY: (800) 659-8331
Website: http://hed.state.nm.us/

New York
New York State Higher Education Services Corporation
99 Washington Avenue
Albany, NY 12255
Phone: (518) 473-1574
Toll-Free: (888) 697-4372
Fax: (518) 474-2839
TTY: (800) 445-5234
Website: http://www.hesc.org/

North Carolina
North Carolina State Education Assistance Authority
P.O. Box 14103
Research Triangle Park, NC 27709
Phone: (919) 549-8614
Toll-Free: (866) 866-2362
Toll-Free restrictions: NC residents only
Fax: (919) 549-8481
Website: http://www.ncseaa.edu/

North Dakota
North Dakota University System
North Dakota Student Financial Assistance Program
600 East Boulevard Avenue, Department 215
Bismarck, ND 58505-0230
Phone: (701) 328-2960
Fax: (701) 328-2961
Website: http://www.ndus.edu/

Ohio
Ohio Board of Regents
State Grants and Scholarships Department
P.O. Box 182452
Columbus, OH 43218-2452

Phone: (614) 466-7420
Toll-Free: (888) 833-1133
Fax: (614) 752-5903
Website: http://regents.ohio.gov/

Oklahoma
Oklahoma State Regents for Higher Education
655 Research Parkway, Suite 200
Oklahoma City, OK 73104
Phone: (405) 225-9100
Toll-Free: (800) 858-1840
Fax: (405) 225-9230
Website: http://www.okhighered.org/

Oregon
Oregon Student Assistance Commission
1500 Valley River Drive, Suite 100
Eugene, OR 97401
Phone: (541) 687-7400
Toll-Free: (800) 452-8807
Fax: (541) 687-7419
Website: http://www.osac.state.or.us/

Pennsylvania
Office of Postsecondary and Higher Education (Pennsylvania)
Department of Education
333 Market Street
Harrisburg, PA 17126
Phone: (717) 787-5041
Fax: (717) 772-3622
TTY: (717) 783-8445
Website: http://www.pdehighered.state.pa.us

Pennsylvania Higher Education Assistance Agency
1200 North Seventh Street
Harrisburg, PA 17102-1444
Phone: (717) 720-2800
Toll-Free: (800) 692-7392

Toll-Free restrictions: PA residents only
Fax: (717) 720-3914
TTY: (800) 654-5988
Website: http://www.pheaa.org/

Puerto Rico
Council on Higher Education (Puerto Rico)
Edificio Hato Rey Center
Avenida Ponce De Leon 268, Suite 1500
San Juan, PR 00918
Phone: (787) 641-7100
Fax: (787) 641-2573
Website: http://www.ces.gobierno.pr/

Rhode Island
Rhode Island Higher Education Assistance Authority
560 Jefferson Boulevard, Suite 100
Warwick, RI 02886-1304
Phone: (401) 736-1100
Toll-Free: (800) 922-9855
Fax: (401) 732-3541
TTY: (401) 734-9481
Website: http://www.riheaa.org/

South Carolina
South Carolina Commission on Higher Education
1333 Main Street, Suite 200
Columbia, SC 29201
Phone: (803) 737-2260
Fax: (803) 737-2297
Website: http://www.che.sc.gov/

South Dakota
Board of Regents (South Dakota)
306 East Capitol Avenue, Suite 200
Pierre, SD 57501-5245
Phone: (605) 773-3455

Fax: (605) 773-5320
Website: http://www.ris.sdbor.edu/

Tennessee
Tennessee Higher Education Commission
Parkway Towers
404 James Robertson Parkway, Suite 1900
Nashville, TN 37243-0830
Phone: (615) 741-3605
Fax: (615) 741-6230
Website: http://www.state.tn.us/thec/

Texas
Texas Higher Education Coordinating Board
P.O. Box 12788
Austin, TX 78711-2788
Phone: (512) 427-6101
Toll-Free: (800) 242-3062
Toll-Free restrictions: Outside Austin metro area
Fax: (512) 427-6127
Website: http://www.thecb.state.tx.us/

Utah
Utah State Board of Regents
Gateway Center
60 South 400 West
Salt Lake City, UT 84101-1284
Phone: (801) 321-7100
Fax: (801) 321-7199
Website: http://www.utahsbr.edu/

Vermont
Vermont Student Assistance Corporation
P.O. Box 2000
Winooski, VT 05404
Phone: (802) 655-9602
Toll-Free: (800) 642-3177

Fax: (802) 654-3765
TTY: (800) 281-3341
Website: http://www.vsac.org/

Virginia
State Council of Higher Education for Virginia
James Monroe Building
101 North 14th Street
Richmond, VA 23219
Phone: (804) 225-2600
Fax: (804) 225-2604
Website: http://www.schev.edu/

Washington
Washington State Higher Education Coordinating Board
P.O. Box 43430
917 Lakeridge Way
Olympia, WA 98504-3430
Phone: (360) 753-7800
Fax: (360) 753-7808
Website: http://www.hecb.wa.gov/

West Virginia
West Virginia Higher Education Policy Commission
1018 Kanawha Boulevard East, Suite 700
Charleston, WV 25301
Phone: (304) 558-2101
Fax: (304) 558-5719
Website: http://www.hepc.wvnet.edu

Wisconsin
Wisconsin Higher Educational Aids Board
131 West Wilson Street, Suite 902
Madison, WI 53703
Phone: (608) 267-2206
Fax: (608) 267-2808
Website: http://heab.state.wi.us/

Wyoming
Wyoming Community College Commission
2020 Carey Avenue, 8th Floor
Cheyenne, WY 82002
Phone: (307) 777-7763
Fax: (307) 777-6567
Website: http://www.commission.wcc.edu/

Glossary

Alumni-Sponsored Scholarship: A scholarship offered by the graduates of a college or university who contributed money to sponsor the scholarship.

Award Criteria: The factors used by judges to determine, among the applicants, who will win the scholarships. (Note the nuances between award and eligibility criteria.)

Community-Service Scholarships: Scholarships based on students' achievements in volunteer work, community organizing, service learning, or other activities that benefit your community.

Disbursement: The payment or transfer of money.

Displacement: Replacing one financial aid resource with another.

Economically Disadvantaged: A status of student or family income. Usually refers to low-income families but could include families who are facing significant financial instability.

Eligibility Criteria: The factors used by sponsors to determine who can apply for their scholarships. (Note the nuances between eligibility and award criteria.)

Estimated Family Contribution (EFC): The amount that the federal government believes your family should contribute to the cost of college, based on the information your family provides and the FAFSA calculations.

Ethnicity-Based Criteria: A factor in eligibility or award criteria that clearly states the ethnicity of the students for whom the scholarship was intended.

Faculty-Sponsored Scholarship: A scholarship funded by the faculty at a university or by faculty within a certain department.

FAFSA Shock: Your family's reaction to the EFC.

Financial Aid: All forms of financial assistance awarded to a student to help pay for college. This includes grants, loans, work-study, and scholarships.

Financial Need: A general term used to capture the many factors that determine family income level and the student's ability to pay for college. The government will provide an estimated family contribution (EFC) after the applicant submits a FAFSA, but scholarship providers may use their own methods of determining need.

Four-Year Scholarship: A sponsor's four-year financial commitment to you.

Free Application for Federal Student Aid (FAFSA): The application required by the federal government to determine if you qualify for need-based aid.

Full-Ride Scholarship: A scholarship whereby the sponsor will pay tuition, room, and board, and in some cases, the entire cost of attendance. It is most likely renewable for four years or until you earn a degree. These are the most coveted, in financial terms, of all scholarships.

Grants: Financial aid that does not need to be paid back. State, federal, tribal, and institutional grants are most common.

Half-Tuition or Full-Tuition Scholarships: The sponsor will award half or all of the "list price" of the tuition at your college. It could be renewable for four years. These scholarships are rare, valuable, and among the most competitive.

Institution-Based Aid: Financial aid distributed from the colleges' own funds or grants they administer for another entity, such as a state agency.

Leadership Scholarships: Scholarships based on students' proven roles as leaders in their schools or communities.

Letter of Recommendation: A letter written by someone who admires you and can testify to your scholarship worthiness.

Merit-Based or Achievement-Based: The primary criteria for a scholarship that is based on academic achievements, possibly measured by GPA, class rank, and test scores.

Minority Scholarships: Scholarships targeting traditionally defined minority groups such as, but not limited to, African-American, Asian-American, Hispanic, Latino, or Native American/American Indian.

Need-Based Aid: Financial aid sources offered to students based on their level of financial need.

Need-Blind: A method whereby funds are awarded without regard to a student's financial needs.

Nomination Form: A document completed by someone who has the power and authority to recommend you for a scholarship. This may or may not accompany letters of recommendation.

One-Time Gift: The sponsor awards the money to the scholarship recipient once. Recipients cannot reapply, because they no longer meet the criteria (incoming freshman) or, as winners, they are prohibited from applying again. These are the most common private scholarships.

Preference: An inclination toward a certain type of student, but if those students don't apply or don't impress the judges, the scholarship committee may select another student.

Preferential Packaging: The practice of using institutional aid (scholarships and grants) to lure or recruit students to a college. Less emphasis is put on self-help aid.

Race-Blind: A method of awarding financial aid whereby race is *not* a factor in eligibility or award criteria.

Renewable Scholarships: Scholarships awarded with the understanding that students may be eligible for another award if they reapply or maintain eligibility, as determined by the sponsor.

Scholarships: Financial aid that is awarded to you based on your individual characteristics. Scholarships do not have to be paid back.

Self-Help Aid: The part of a financial aid package that is the student's responsibility, such as loans and work-study.

Standardized Tests: Tests meant to measure your college readiness in terms of your level of achievement or aptitude. The ACT and SAT are the major tests. The test scores may be used by colleges during the admissions process and by scholarship providers during the application process.

Student Loans: Financial aid that is offered to you based on the shortfall between what you have and what you owe toward the cost of college. Loans accrue interest and must be repaid.

Traditionally Underrepresented Group: Students who, historically, have not enrolled in a particular college or program.

Transcript: A school's or school district's official record of a student's courses and grades.

Tuition Discounting: Financial aid practice whereby colleges and universities reduce the price of tuition to recruit highly desirable students.

Work-Study: A need-based financial aid program whereby colleges provide jobs to students. The wages are subsidized by the federal government, the college, and sometimes by the state.

Index

Note: Page numbers in italics refer to illustrations.

*Because a stellar education alone isn't always enough
to ensure success . . .*

25 Ways to Make College Pay Off
Advice for Anxious Parents from a Professor Who's Seen It All

By Bill Coplin, Ph.D.

In the next few years, parents can expect to spend more than $40,000 per year on their child's college tuition. While that number may seem frightening, it is not as grim as the statistics that predict their child's chances of actually finding a job after graduation. Only about 20% of employers believe college graduates are ready for the workforce, and only 40% of graduates will find a job that will ensure their financial independence. The good news is that with the right advice, parents can turn their pricey investment into one that truly yields a high return and a rewarding career for their son or daughter. Professor Coplin offers honest advice for parents who want their child's college experience to ensure future success—both financially and emotionally. Parents will learn how to help their college-bound student:

- Develop skills employers actually want
- Get their first job
- Treat career services as their best ally
- Explore a variety of career paths
- Realize the importance of the unpaid internship
- And more

A unique and no-nonsense blueprint, *25 Ways to Make College Pay Off* will show parents how to mentor and guide their child through college so that he or she gets the most out of the experience and leaves prepared for the real world.

Paperback ISBN 978-0-8144-7456-3 $14.95

AMACOM Books www.amacombooks.org
